# The Who
## and
# The Why

# The Who and The Why

Ben Fisher

Why Publishing

Copyright © 2021 by Ben Fisher

All rights reserved. No part of this book may be reproduced in any manner whatsoever without written permission except in the case of brief quotations embodied in critical articles and reviews.

First Printing, 2021

ISBN: 978-1-8383531-0-0


Unless otherwise stated, Scripture quotations are from the ESV® Bible (The Holy Bible, English Standard Version®), copyright © 2001 by Crossway, a publishing ministry of Good News Publishers. Used by permission. All rights reserved.

Scripture quotations [marked NIV] taken from the Holy Bible, New International Version Anglicised Copyright © 1979, 1984, 2011 Biblica

Used by permission of Hodder & Stoughton Ltd, an Hachette UK Company.

All rights reserved.

'NIV' is a registered trademark of Biblica UK trademark number 1448790.

My thanks to, Derek Johnson and Liz Thomas for all of their valuable time spent in reading through, encouraging and offering suggestions to make this book better. To Alun for his meticulous eye in weeding out many grammatical mistakes that both man and software had previously missed.

My thanks also, to my wonderful wife Tracy, who not only read through this book giving helpful feedback, but also graciously put up with all of my time that it took up. Finally, my deepest thanks to God for the blessings that He has and continues to work in me through the truths contained in this book. If only I wasn't such a slow learner.

# Contents

| | |
|---|---|
| Introduction | 1 |
| Chapter 1 – These Three Remain | 3 |
| Chapter 2 – Ditches | 11 |
| Chapter 3 – Labels, Sails & Crutches | 19 |
| Chapter 4 – Faith | 31 |
| Chapter 5 – Hope | 65 |
| Chapter 6 – Love | 97 |
| Chapter 7 – The Who and The Why | 131 |
| Chapter 8 – Daydreaming With God | 143 |

# Introduction

Why? That's often the question, isn't it? Children to parents, us to God, and probably more often than we realise God to us. Why? God is as keen if not more so, on the motives or the heart behind our actions than the actions themselves. Now don't twist that statement in your mind. We'll come across a few statements like this throughout the book, and to say 'This' is more important than 'That' is not to say that 'That' is unimportant. Your thoughts, words and actions are of great importance, but behind them all are your desires, your reasoning, your motivations – in short, 'The why'.

When I went to University to study mechanical engineering, in the final design module I was given the chance to design essentially whatever I wanted – as long as I got approval from the lecturer, and to my genuine surprise, my idea was given the go-ahead. I wanted to design an 'uncomfortable bed'. The thinking was this, if you're like me, sometimes (almost always) you may find it hard to get out of bed in the mornings. This is because the bed seems so much more desirable than the outside world. Now, as a training engineer, there is little I could do to affect how you feel about what you are waking up to, whatever that may be, but I can make the bed less desirable - hence the 'uncomfortable bed'. At a set time, instead of, or as well as an alarm going off, the bed would change shape and become uncomfortable. The design was simple, a pole would be inserted underneath the mattress approximately halfway down the bed spanning across it, and this would be lifted so that the occupant would now be lying on an apex roof shape mattress. We tested this very scientifically of course. With the aid of one of my housemates, who kindly agreed to be experimented on, we slid a long broom handle across underneath the mattress and lifted it in the middle, testing different heights to find the right balance between being uncomfortable and not breaking his back. (In case you're interested we reckoned approximately 10 cm was about the right height).

This was a not so serious attempt at working with the desires and motivations within us, but the truth is this: that as a rule, we will do what we most desire to do, what we are the most motivated to do (within what we feel we are able to do). This is one reason why as God works in you His primary method and objective is not to change your actions, but to change your heart, your motivations – 'The why'.

~ 1 ~

# These three remain

It's got to be a contender for the most misquoted verse in the Bible and comes right after one of the most popular and well-known passages: *"Love is patient, love is kind. It does not envy, it does not boast, it is not proud. It does not dishonour others, it is not self-seeking, it is not easily angered, it keeps no record of wrongs. Love does not delight in evil but rejoices with the truth. It always protects, always trusts, always hopes, always perseveres."*[1a] Brilliant, wonderful words, and there we should pause, but quite often we plough on ignoring the punctuation and finish with... *"Love never fails."*[1b]

But these words do not end the previous paragraph; they start the next one where they take on their different and intended meaning...

> *"Love never ends. As for prophecies, they will pass away, as for tongues, they will cease; as for knowledge, it will pass away. For we know in part and we prophesy in part, but when the perfect comes, the partial will pass away. When I was a child, I spoke like a child, I thought like a child, I*

1. (a-b) 1 Cor 13:4-8 NIV

> *reasoned like a child. When I became a man, I gave up childish ways. For now we see in a mirror dimly, but then face to face. Now I know in part; then I shall know fully, even as I have been fully known. So now faith, hope, and love abide, these three; but the greatest of these is love."*

1 Cor 13:8-13

Love never ends, as some translations perhaps more helpfully put it. That is to say that its existence and purpose never ends. When this life ends and God is seen, not just as in a dull reflection but fully for all He is, there will be no more need for the gifts of prophecy and tongues, they will pass away and be replaced by a fuller knowledge of the glory and wonder of God. But love, well this is different, love is fundamentally and equally important in this life as it is in the one to come.

This is not to reduce the value of prophecy or tongues, in this very same book, indeed the very next sentence[2] Paul encourages a desire for Spiritual gifts - especially prophecy. Rather Paul is writing to a church where there is an over-emphasis on the gifts, which is both coming from and feeding wrong attitudes: "look at me – I can do this, I'm more important than you". He's trying to re-balance their thoughts and priorities because the truth is God is more interested in the person you're becoming than what you do, or what you've done - good or bad.

Love, Faith and Hope could be described as 'the three imperishables' – these you can take with you. They have as

---

2.  1 Cor 14:1

much purpose and value in the next life as they do in this one, and they are the three main motivational characteristics that God wants to infuse into the core of your very being. God desires to grow each of us more and more into the likeness of His Son Jesus Christ[3], but this doesn't mean He's out to make us all into identical clones. The irrepressible, infinite worth and wonder of God will never be fully expressed in any single one of us, and neither is it supposed to be. We were made in His image, but He alone is God. And you were never intended to be exactly the same as anybody else, you are unique and handcrafted by the Master Builder. But consistent throughout each and every one of us is His desire to imbed in the core of your soul these three things to define who you are and motivate what you do: Faith, Hope and Love, and the greatest of these is Love.

## *'The who'*

I was reminded a while ago of a quote from Dr Paul Brand concerning his mother: *"This is how to grow old. Allow everything else to fall away, until those around you see just love."*[4] Now there's a danger with quotes like this that they can come across a little trite or soppy, but not when you know the story behind it, of this life well lived, then it gains some gravity and we'll look at her story later in the book. But before that, when I was reminded of this quote it set off some God prompted self-examination. Mentally I

---

3. Rom 8:29
4. Dorothy Clarke Wilson, Granny Brand Her Story, P206, 1976

wasn't in a great place; I had at that time been going down that often un-helpful road of comparing myself to others, whether that be achievements, the stuff I have, the stage in life I'd gotten too. At the time I worked as a self-employed bathroom fitter (I still do as I write this) and had done for several years. Business was not great, I was surviving but little more, and I was becoming more and more aware of the financial gap between myself and those I knew who were in employment. Some of them would tell me how they wished they were self-employed so that they could be their own boss, and indeed there are many potential benefits. But whereas they saw the benefits for me and moaned about the harder parts of their jobs, I saw the drawbacks in my situation and the benefits in theirs - having a consistent salary over the months and years, paid holidays and sick leave... Yes, yes, I know – the grass is always greener...

But that wasn't really the problem, there will always be pros and cons to this sort of thing. The problem was that I had let my self-worth start to attach itself to these things. I was a good bathroom fitter, but not a great businessman, and after seven or so years I had little to show for the business I had started. And as I looked around, I saw many people better funded, with homes they were paying off, the beginnings of pension funds, and who simply looked to be more successful in what they did than me. I was still renting and unable to get a mortgage, no pension, little savings, and as far as I could see not much to show for my years of work.

But God wasn't going to let me wallow in this for long, and very soon came the first 'prod of God' through the quote above: "This is how to grow old. Allow everything else to fall away, until those around you see just love." I don't remember what God used to bring this to mind, I've heard it from several sources over the years, but God used it to set off a series of thoughts.

First came simply the realisation of how unhealthy my mind was in focusing on these things – they do have importance but they're not what life is all about, nor is my worth tied to them. I wasn't able to simply flick a switch and deal with it, but I was now alert enough to start tackling the thoughts head-on when they arose. However, I then followed a path of new comparisons. Evelyn "Granny" Brand is the lady being spoken of in the quote above. I love her story and hearing it led me to assess my life afresh but with new parameters. I was no longer comparing stuff I had or successfulness in business, I was comparing my growth in character, not with Evelyn Brand – I was switched on enough by this point to be inspired by her life, not depressed by the gulf between our characters. No, rather I was comparing my character and my growth in my relationship with God, over the previous 10 years. This did depress me! Sure I was a little wiser than 10 years ago, but had my relationship with God developed at all? Not really, if anything I was treating it as less precious than I used to, and my actions and attitude showed it. I remembered a phrase I heard a preacher use: 'feeding leftovers to a hungry God'.

Ouch – that really gut punched me the first time I heard it, but not nearly enough. I discovered that I'd had that same type of attitude for many years. Oh, I kept in 'regular contact' with God over those years, but really, He wasn't the priority that He should have been or deserved. And had I been growing in Faith, Hope and Love? In some ways maybe yes, in others definitely no.

I used to be told that I had wisdom beyond my years. Now part of the problem with that is if you hear it too many times you might start believing it too much, then pride comes in and has its ugly way. But worse still is the realisation of the years catching up and probably overtaking the wisdom. As one of my friends likes to say "with age comes wisdom – but sometimes age shows up by itself".

For a while I let myself fall further into self-pity – a failure on all fronts; where it doesn't matter so much, and where it really does! But God was not done with me and quickly snapped me out of it. I found then that I knew three things very clearly; First, that God loved me, and that this love was undiminished by my failings. Secondly, that He was not finished with me. And thirdly, that He was inviting me to step up and work with Him hand in hand as He seeks to grow me into the person He made me to be.

So here's what you need to understand; your life is primarily God's project, not yours. And he's far more concerned that you reach your full potential than you are. Oh, you'll have different ideas from Him as to the best route travelled, timetable, and yes, most likely even the final outcome. He has many tools and many methods, most subtle and some anything but – but all of them working for your good. I love how John Ortberg talks about this; he says, that as God works in you *"You don't just become Holier. You become You-ier,"*[5] You become more like the person God made you to be. God is more interested in the person you're becoming than what you do, or what you've done - good and bad. Take heart, God is a completer/finisher, and He will finish what He started in you[6].

## *More or less*

Let me take another brief moment to address a problem I've sometimes come across. Occasionally I find that when you declare something to be more important, what gets heard is that the other thing is unimportant! This is not what I'm saying here. What you do, and what you've done is significant, whether the good that God delights in or the bad that grieves Him – it all matters. It affects your life, other's lives, and your relationship with God for better or worse. But when God saved you, when He sent His Son to die in your place taking on the punishment of sin, He didn't just finish something, He started something: a new work – in you, and He's working still. Not to teach you to simply speak and act and in a different way but to be different, to change you from within.

5. John Ortberg, The Me I Want To Be, P16, 2010
6. Php 1:6

The good you've done in the past, that's great. The bad, well there's no getting around it, you're not supposed to feel okay about that. Let it humble you, and increase your thankfulness and dependence on God's grace. But none of it defines you. Primarily God is working not to change your actions (though these are important) but your core character and motivations – the 'Who' and the 'Why'. There are many aspects to this, but I believe at the core of this, are these three motivational characteristics: faith, hope and love. These form the foundation and fountain out of which so many other things flow.

> *"The good person out of the good treasure of his heart produces good, and the evil person out of his evil treasure produces evil, for out of the abundance of the heart his mouth speaks."*

Luke 6:45

# ~2~

# Ditches

In the following chapters we'll go on to look more closely at faith, hope and love each in turn and see what it looks like to be characterised and motivated by them. But first I want to consider another 'why' – why bother?

The path that God has laid out for us to walk as Christians always seems to have ditches on either side, errors we can make which pull us away from God's desire for our lives. Frustratingly, recognising the error we're making on one side can sometimes lead to an overreaction, in turn leading to an over-correction that just lands us in the ditch on the other side. In the third chapter in Philippians Paul seems to be addressing one such example of this. In this case, self-reliance vs idleness. It's a 'classic' and common problem, and for my part, I must confess I've spent time in both ditches, but mostly in the idleness one.

Paul is keen that the Philippians should *"Look out for the dogs, look out for the evildoers, look out for those who mutilate the flesh"* [1] for those who were trying to lay a weight on Christians never intended for them – physical circumcision. *"For we are the circumcision, who worship*

1. Php 3:2

*by the Spirit of God and glory in Christ Jesus and put no confidence in the flesh"* [2]. It seems that some of the Jewish Christians were trying to bring in and enforce a ritual God never intended for the Christian believer. Circumcision was part of the old covenant, not the new one. Paul was keen to show that the new covenant God made was not looking for a physical change or symbol but a change of heart. 'However, if you want to talk about works and achievements made in the flesh to earn your way to God, check this out', says Paul: *"If anyone else thinks he has reason for confidence in the flesh, I HAVE MORE: circumcised on the eighth day, of the people of Israel, of the tribe of Benjamin, a Hebrew of Hebrews; as to the law, a Pharisee; as to zeal, a persecutor of the church; as to righteousness under the law, blameless."* [3] You can't accuse Paul of being shy or timid. 'What do you think you have?' Paul challenges them, 'because I guarantee I can trump it!'

And yet this is not where Paul's faith, joy and security lies – *"But whatever gain I had, I counted as loss for the sake of Christ. Indeed, I count everything as loss because of the surpassing worth of knowing Christ Jesus my Lord. For his sake I have suffered the loss of all things and count them as rubbish, in order that I may gain Christ and be found in him, not having a righteousness of my own that comes from the law, but that which comes through faith in Christ, the righteousness from God that depends on faith..."* [4] Paul could rattle you off a long list of reason's he could claim for being confident in his flesh – that is, all he's achieved

2. Php 3:3
3. Php 3:4-6
4. Php 3:7-9

through simply his birthright and in turn his zeal and his accomplishments. But he's having none of it, he counts them as loss, as rubbish. When he talks about suffering loss here it's not about 'stuff', or about all the comforts and possessions he gave up to follow Christ in the way he did. He's talking about rejecting his previously perceived right to boast – all the aspects of his life that looked like he was a man of high esteem, a man earning his place before God. And he's not just rejecting these things, what was once considered to his profit and helpful, he's counting them as loss, as liabilities. Paul had spent much of his life in the ditch of self-reliance, and he wanted to save his readers from falling into the same ditch. Or to change the imagery slightly, into the rut of self-reliance. And as you may have heard it said: 'a rut is simply a grave with the ends knocked out'. There's no life there.

Now Paul starts to transition his teaching to deal with the other ditch or rut: ... *"that I may know him and the power of his resurrection, and may share his sufferings, becoming like him in his death, THAT BY ANY MEANS POSSIBLE I MAY ATTAIN the resurrection from the dead. Not that I have already obtained this or am already perfect, but I PRESS ON to make it my own, because Christ Jesus has made me his own. Brothers, I do not consider that I have made it my own. But one thing I do: forgetting what lies behind and STRAINING FORWARD to what lies ahead, I PRESS ON toward the goal for the prize of the upward call of God in Christ Jesus."* [5] Listen to the language repeated

5.   Php 3:10-14 (Emphasis mine)

here again and again: 'pressing on, straining forwards'. Paul is no idle man, he hasn't put his faith and trust in Christ Jesus to then simply sit back and do nothing. That phrase you sometimes hear of 'let go and let God' is right and good used in its right setting, such as relying entirely on Him to pay the cost of your sins. But in other places, it's not always helpful or biblical! Certainly here, directly after emphasising how he doesn't rely on his own works, he isn't now talking about sitting back and letting God do all the work, no Pauls rallying cry is 'Rely on God and press forwards!' This same principle is repeated in 2 Timothy 2:7 where he says "Think over what I say…" (action/effort), "… for the Lord will give you understanding in everything" (relying on God). Act Timothy! Put the effort in, for you can be sure God will respond and give you what you need.

How many of us in the church today can really say that we're striving forwards? I know that for my own part I've spent far too much time balancing on the edge of the ditch of idleness, if not face splat down in it! This is not a contradiction of the perils found in the ditch of self-reliance. Paul's not trying to earn anything here, his motivation is found in the first verse of chapter 3 in Philippian's – joy, he wants to know God and the fullness of life found in Him alone, even if that means suffering. He doesn't just want a certificate that gets him into heaven, but he desires to press on, leaving the way of life behind that Jesus saved him from, and straining ever forwards into the type of life that he was saved for. Put simply, to grow ever closer into the kind of person God made him to be. A person wholeheartedly in love with God and devoted to His ways. Doesn't that sound good to you?

Consider this, as a parent I've often got little 'helpers' wanting to get in on the action, be it household jobs (yes mine as I write this are still young enough to think it's fun to 'help' with that), cake making, gardening... Any of these things would be far easier and quicker if I did them myself. But through involving them, I'm helping them to grow and learn far better than if I did it myself, and our relationship with each other develops as we do it together. Now, if He chose to, God could click his proverbial fingers and simply make us a completely new and fully formed person now. That He doesn't choose to do this tells me that He knows there's a better way. And that way seems to be one where we 'help', where we get involved in what He's doing, whilst He makes the difference and makes sure the house actually gets cleaned, that the cake will taste great, and that the garden will flourish. Plus all the while we're learning and spending quality time with our precious Heavenly Father.

### *Subtleties*

It's interesting to me how subtle the fall into either of these ditches can be, and how similar the outward signs can be. You don't need to be forcefully insisting that everyone needs to be circumcised to fall into the ditch of self-reliance, neither do you need to be a couch potato waiting for the end to be in the ditch of idleness.

In the end, it's all about attitude, the motivations or indeed 'the why'. The ditch of self-reliance tends to show itself in the form of 'Christ plus'. Yes, Jesus died on the cross for me, and to make sure I'm all ok with the 'big guy above', I'm going to Church every Sunday, giving 10% of my earnings, I read my Bible every day, say grace before meals, pray regularly and have cut out swearing altogether… All good things. All great things actually, but if they're being done to earn anything before God, or to earn your place among those saved by Christ you're misunderstanding what God has truly done for you, and how your relationship with him has changed. It's a scarily subtle difference shown only in the heart attitude, where, with your lips, you declare Christ is all you need, but in your heart, you're doing these things to try and earn the love He has shown.

Intriguingly, the person in the other ditch (of idleness), might present with pretty much the same initial outer appearance, but instead of an attitude of 'Christ plus', or earning anything before God, it's more of a tick box mentality:

'Right then; weekly church attendance, tick; regular (or occasional) prayer and bible study, tick; giving money to the church and my monthly sponsorship of an orphaned child, tick. Right, that should be enough. I can do what I like with the rest of my time.'

There's no attempt to earn anything before God, you feel certain that what He did was enough to save you – great! But you also feel like you've done enough to honour and mark Christ's death and resurrection. You feel assured that He's saved you from your sins and your old way of life, but don't feel at all motivated to discover the fulness of life He has saved you *for* now, not just in the age to come. Does that really honour God, are you truly content to leave it there?

I encourage you to take time out and ask God to expose your heart. You could be doing many things that outwardly look good, and yet you're still slap face down in the mud of one ditch or the other. The 'why' is so important, and God would encourage us to strive, to press on towards the goal, towards the life He wants for us. Developing that intimate relationship with Him every step along the way, as we rely on Him to always make the ultimate difference. To be the One who truly makes it happen.

~3~

# Labels, Sails & Crutches

Labels, we do like to label and categorise things don't we? Make a neat box to put them in. This can be both helpful and unhelpful at times, so before we delve into a deeper look at faith, hope and love I want to explain why I've labelled them as 'motivational characteristics', and why I think it's helpful to think of them this way.

I wish I could point out a few parts of scripture and say 'look, this is how the Bible categorises them', but it doesn't do this. The only reason that I started to look for one, is because of how often they're brought up together, or sometimes just two of them at a time. It seems that faith, hope and love appear to be in a class of their own, and I was intrigued to try and see what linked them – why it's these three things that 'remain'.

My conclusion came in part from a process of elimination, and the easiest way to see this is to look at love. I don't know about you, but I often hear teachings about love not being a mere feeling? And I agree, when the Bible talks about loving people, it talks about actions towards others. So cross off feelings – faith, hope and love are not feelings or emotions (though they have a huge effect on them). But what often comes next when this is taught is that love is therefore a choice or an action. Now there's some truth in this and it is helpful to take us away from the thought that love is all about the thrill and the emotions, but I can't help but feel this is an uncompleted thought process. The Bible tells us that "man looks on the outward appearance, but the LORD looks on the heart."[1] Now I know in its context that this is comparing how we may look at someone's bodily appearance when God looks at the heart, but it begins to show us a principle. So consider this: in 1 Corinthian's 13:1-3 we're told:

> *"If I speak in the tongues of men and of angels, but have not love, I am a noisy gong or a clanging cymbal. And if I have prophetic powers, and understand all mysteries and all knowledge, and if I have all faith, so as to remove mountains, but have not love, I am nothing. If I give away all I have, and if I deliver up my body to be burned, but have not love, I gain nothing."*

You can give all - everything you own, all your money and possessions to the poor, and yet do it without any love in your heart! It even talks about surrendering your body to be burned – I presume it's talking about for God's sake, thinking of those who have died rather than deny Him? So we have an example of what would surely be considered an extreme loving act towards others, followed by an example

---

1. 2 Sam 16:7

of what might be considered an ultimate act of love towards God, and yet all done without love! Love is not an action.

So having eliminated love as being a feeling or an action the conclusion I often hear is that love is a choice. I have some sympathy for this thinking but ultimately believe that love lies a step deeper within. Love is seen in the choice because love was the *motivator*, the reason the choice was made – the why. Just as we saw above with actions, you could make a set of choices that all appear loving and yet have been motivated by something else entirely. As I write this, my wedding anniversary is coming up, now imagine the day arriving and I've bought my wife some lovely flowers and a gift, to which she responds: "Oh you shouldn't have." Imagine if my heart's reply was 'yes I should – it's what a husband is supposed to do on an anniversary.' Does that sound like love to you? How about if my heart's reply is 'but I wanted to – I know it makes you happy' That's surely more like it. Love has motivated me, pushed me on to find time to think about and buy the gift and flowers. If it's come out of duty that will start to show sooner or later, and my wife would rightly start to feel less loved.

Even if not straight away, people tend to realise when actions are coming out of love or not. I have heard non-Christian's complain of feeling like they're merely a project for their Christian friend, that whatever nice things they do for them or fun stuff they invite them too there's an ulterior motive – recruitment! And you know what, I'm sure some of the time they're absolutely right. I've sat through plenty of teaching about 'friendship evangelism' (which is brilliant and should be taught), but where the motivation taught alongside it (or at least that comes across) is not love, but numbers and duty. Now, this was not necessarily done entirely consciously, but I know I'm not the only one who felt this way. I suspect that most of those that prove to be particularly good at evangelism, especially 'friendship evangelism', don't just go at it with a particular skill set or anointing, but with a genuine and deep-felt heart for the lost – they really care about the people they meet and desperately want to see them made right with God. And this comes across. Indeed, maybe part of the anointing is this genuine loving heart for the lost?

## *Commanding the 'un-commandable'?*

One objection that might arise in all this is that you can't force or manufacture a motivation. So, when Jesus tells us the greatest commandment is to love the Lord our God with all that we are, and to love others as ourselves, that would mean He's commanding the un-commandable? I have some sympathy for this argument, but ultimately don't we find that without God's continuing working within us, we can and do fall short of any given command? Having been saved and justified by Jesus dying in our place and raising to life again, we're now called to live holy lives like

His. Not through our own strength and striving, but through striving alongside Him - relying on the work of the Holy Spirit within us as we learn to keep in step with Him. Or to put it in theologian speak: having been saved and justified by His grace, we need to go on being sanctified by His grace. We remain dependant on Him. So I have no problem in affirming that in a sense God commands the 'un-commandable' in His greatest commandment, because ever since that first sin by Adam and Eve in the garden of Eden we've been in a position where we are simply unable to live up to God's just and perfect standards. We're simply not strong enough in and of ourselves, and our desires so often lead us away from Him instead of towards Him. Our only option for long term change and meaningful holiness is to push forwards with His strength holding us up. For He really does command what is impossible for us in our natural sinful state, and then He works with us and in us to make it possible.

So what's our role in all this? How do we grow, particularly in faith, hope and love?

### *Sailing lessons*

I was blessed to grow up during my teenage years near a popular place to learn how to sail in England – Lymington on the south coast. At that time I was able to get sailing lessons for just £1 a week! And no, I'm not old enough for that to be a lot of money in those days - we're only talking about the latter part of the 1990's. And on top of that, the doughnuts that one of the kind ladies made and brought in most weeks were more than worth the £1 in my eyes (and belly). Only being allowed one doughnut each time made it a painful (and enforced) lesson in self-control, but my main regret is that it wasn't till around twenty years later that I came across an illustration concerning sailing and the Holy Spirit, which has really helped me.

In Ephesians 5:15-18 it says:

> *"Look carefully then how you walk, not as unwise but as wise, making the best use of the time, because the days are evil. Therefore do not be foolish, but understand what the will of the Lord is. And do not get drunk with wine, for that is debauchery, but be filled with the Spirit..."*

On several occasions, I've had this verse quoted to me and have been encouraged to view being filled with the Spirit (repeatedly and continuously as the Greek implies), as something where I just need to pick up a glass of Holy Spirit and drink. Now I have friends that have found this genuinely helpful, so I don't completely begrudge it by any means, but for myself, it could barely have been less helpful. And I'm not convinced that's quite what the author is saying – i.e. don't pick up a glass of wine, instead here have this glass of Holy Spirit. The Holy Spirit is alive and active, personable, and indeed a person! And more to the point there is not a physical glass of Him in front of me to pick up and drink. Neither does it help me to picture Him this way and then do it on some spiritual level. If it's helped you – great, I'm not saying it's wrong, I'm genuinely pleased and have friends who also found it helpful. But if you're awkward like me, and it hasn't helped you, try this way of looking at it:

Consider the Holy Spirit being like a wind. He is active, and on the move, but more importantly, moving in a specific direction. He is purposeful, and not just meandering around waiting for someone to engage with Him. So the question we need to be frequently asking Him is: "where are you 'blowing' today?" Or: "what work are you doing in both my life and in those around me?" When sailing you make much more progress if the wind is behind you and you're traveling in the same direction as the wind. Oh, you can go against it if you want to, but to do that, you have to keep 'tacking' (turning) side to side every so often, and so you get to your destination by traveling in a zigzag.

Going with the wind

⟶

Going against the wind

It's not that you can't do it, indeed it's still through the power found in the wind that progress is made, but it's far harder and progress is much slower.

Now in sailing it's an important skill to learn – well vital really, you generally don't just keep sailing where the wind is blowing, you need to be able to get back again. But with the Spirit the skill or the attitude we need to develop is about going along with Him – discerning where He is working, where He is blowing, so that we can put out our sail and be filled with Him and moved by His power. A sail boat is quite ineffective without wind, and so are we without Him. But if we can learn to daily check where He is active and what He is doing, then we can raise our sails and make full use of the power found through Him.

I also like this illustration because it also draws in other aspects that we are taught in this part of Ephesians:

> *"Look carefully then how you walk, not as unwise but as wise, making the best use of the time, because the days are evil. Therefore do not be foolish, but understand what the will of the Lord is..."*

Eph 5:15-17.

We're encouraged to walk wisely, making the best use of the time, understanding what the Lord's will is. To me, that is all encompassed in this picture of seeking to understand where the Holy Spirit is blowing, and so directing our lives and raising our sails to be filled by Him and go where He goes, to work where He is working through His power.

There are so many ways we could all grow in maturity as Christians. I could write you a long list detailing my failings, but focusing on everything at once is overwhelming – and as far as I can see it's not how God tends to work. So as we seek to grow as Christian's we need to be regularly asking The Holy Spirit: which area/s of my character are you working on at the moment? And then get alongside Him and put our efforts into the same area/s.

## *Crutches*

So then, how do we work on our motivations? How can we alter or grow something so fundamental to who we are? Having identified where God is working in us I'd suggest four steps:

First – Pray for help in making the change happen (no surprise there).

Secondly – Learn what the real thing looks like. If you don't understand your target it's going to be much harder to work towards and hit it. That's what the next few chapters are for – looking at faith, hope and love individually to become familiar with what they look like, how they feel, what kind of results we get from having them characterise us and motivate our lives. And though we are so often a mix of a variety of motivations running at the same time, to separate them out for a moment will be helpful.

Thirdly – Regularly think about the truths found in the Bible that encourage and give life to these characteristics.

And finally – We need to learn how to use appropriate crutches.

> *"A perfect man would never act from a sense of duty; he'd always want the right thing more than the wrong one. Duty is only a substitute for love (of God and other people) like a crutch which is a substitute for a leg. Most of us need the crutch at times; but of course it is idiotic to use the crutch when our own legs (our own loves, tastes, habits etc.) can do the journey on their own."* [2]
>
> C.S. Lewis

Part of training ourselves and seeking to grow these motivations will come in simply mimicking the results, and doing what we know they should result in. This could be something as simple as spending a little extra quality time with the kids when what you really want to do is go and have a bit of time to yourself. Then try and absorb the good it does and the worth there is in pushing through. As we do these things we need to be honest with ourselves and with God about where the motivation came from, otherwise we risk covering over a weaker area of our lives and think we're in a better place than we are. More to the point, we risk being false. The goal of using a crutch should always be

---

2. C.S. Lewis (2003), A Mind Awake: An Anthology Of C.S. Lewis, p142 Houghton Mifflin Harcourt

to get the leg/motivation strong enough to carry the weight by itself. Not to pretend or deceive ourselves.

In Hebrews 12:11 when talking about God disciplining His children it says that the result is a harvest of *"the peaceful fruit of righteousness for those who are trained by it"*. The good that can come from trials and discipline in all its forms is not automatic. It comes only to those who engage with and are trained by it. Similarly, we could use our crutches without being trained by it, and so not reap the benefits. It needs to be a conscious, unrushed and prayerful thing.

~4~

# Faith

So what exactly is faith? We use the word in a variety of ways, for example, we tend to mean something a little different when we say that someone is 'full of faith' as opposed to being 'faithful' (though they are strongly linked). We speak of 'The Faith' and 'blind leaps of faith'. Indeed people put their faith in a variety of things, be it the strength of the materials used in a building or a bridge they're crossing, or perhaps the competence of the people who designed and built it. We put our faith in businesses to do and carry out different tasks, like keeping us supplied with water and electricity or turning up when they say they will. We put our faith in our friends to be there when we need them. All these things are good, but they're not what we're talking about here. Just as it will be with hope and love, the faith we're talking about is a God-centered faith, and it should be no surprise that we'll find that for each of these the source is found in Him and that its presence in our lives will make our reflection of Him that little bit clearer.

In a film called Serenity, a kind of space/western written and directed by Joss Whedon, we find its main character, Mal, on the run from a sinister government agent. Mal flees to his old friend Shepherd Book, who has given Mal both advice and shelter in the past, only to find that Book and the children he looks after have been slaughtered. As Shepherd Book lays there dying he gives his final words of advice: "I don't care what you believe, just believe." In what is otherwise a well written film this key emotional moment falls a little flat because it simply just doesn't make sense. In fact the rest of the film shows exactly why: by this point much has already been made of how the unnamed agent 'believes hard' and part of his strength is in that. But his belief has clearly put him on the wrong side and led him to do awful things including the murder of Book and all those children. Furthermore, by the end, he comes to see how his faith has been misplaced in the regime he blindly and secretly upheld. So the film as a whole shows how silly such a comment truly is. Believing in something/anything is not what really matters. What matters is *what* we believe, or more to the point, who we put our faith in.

Now our base camp for exploring faith will be the well-known section from the book of Hebrews. From here we will gather a variety of things about the faith that God wants to infuse into us. It will not be exhaustive and there's much more that can be learned, but we will end up with a couple of simple truths that I believe helpfully summarise what faith in God looks like and the way that this God-centered faith affects and motivates us.

## *Assurance and Conviction*

*"Now faith is the assurance of things hoped for, the conviction of things not seen."*

*Hebrews 11:1*

Straight away we hit something very important about faith but easily rushed over; faith is about assurance, substance, and conviction – certainty. In the world Faith can often be portrayed as an 'airy-fairy' type thing; "it's where (bless them) they believe (though there's no evidence) about something the rest of us clued up people don't..." But this is not how the Bible talks about faith, it uses words like conviction, or as some translations put it, evidence! Faith is the evidence of things not seen. We're not encouraged to believe in something, or indeed someone, with no evidence to support this belief. We hear the gospel about Jesus Christ, we read His Word and we are convicted to our core, we both see and hear the truth of what is being taught. We may not physically see God, but we can see evidence of Him literally everywhere. In Romans, Paul affirms that *"...His invisible attributes, namely, his eternal power and divine nature, have been clearly perceived, ever since the creation of the world, in the things that have been made."*[1] It's not just that through faith we can see this, but also that in our physical seeing and experience of creation our faith is affirmed and formed. And though many try to tell us otherwise it is all evidence of God.

1. Rom 1:20

Furthermore, when we come to faith in Christ, our faith is strengthened all the more as we find that we have *"received the Spirit of adoption as sons, by whom we cry, "Abba! Father!" The Spirit himself bears witness with our spirit that we are children of God."*[2] We may not be able to prove it to those around us, but to receive The Holy Spirit and have His affirming presence in our lives is such great evidence of the reality of God that it can't help but build up our faith. It is all evidence, and it results in conviction and certainty in what is unseen. Or to put it another way - faith!

### Miss-spelt?

At the time of writing I hadn't heard this said for quite a while, so hopefully it's been left behind now, but in the past, I've heard it said from quite a few places that "faith is spelt R.I.S.K." Now I understand why this is taught and there is a great golden nugget of truth in it, which we'll unpack later on in this chapter, but it's unhelpfully leaping ahead of itself. No, if anything faith is spelt S.U.R.E. Remember it's about certainty and conviction, and it's really important that we start with this.

---

2. Rom 8:15-16

## FAITH 35

### *The Core of the Matter:*

> *"...without faith it is impossible to please him, for whoever would draw near to God must believe that he exists and that he rewards those who seek him."*
>
> Hebrews 11:5-6

Without faith it is impossible to please God. Just let that sink in a moment. Without faith you'll never please Him – it's simply impossible. And we're immediately told why, so the rest of that sentence is telling us key things about faith. Now I almost feel silly writing this as it's surely stating the obvious, but it's right there in the Bible to be said: a key part of faith is believing that God exists. It's as simple as that, and of course, you're not going to please anyone if you don't even acknowledge that they exist. But it's more than that, as James puts it in his letter *"Even the demons believe – and shudder!"*[3] Faith in God isn't just about believing that He exists but carries with it a desire to draw near to God, and a belief that there are rewards in seeking Him – that He is both worthy and worth it!

Jesus taught that:

> *"The kingdom of heaven is like treasure hidden in a field. When a man found it, he hid it again, and then in his joy went and sold all he had and bought that field."*

---

3. James 2:19

> *"Again, the kingdom of heaven is like a merchant looking for fine pearls. When he found one of great value, he went away and sold everything he had and bought it"*
>
> Matt 13:44-46 NIV

And again:

> *"For which of you, desiring to build a tower, does not first sit down and count the cost, whether he has enough to complete it? Otherwise, when he has laid a foundation and is not able to finish, all who see it begin to mock him, saying, 'This man began to build and was not able to finish.'... So therefore, any one of you who does not renounce all that he has cannot be my disciple."*
>
> Luke 14: 28-29,33

God is looking for people who believe in Him, and believe that there is reward in seeking Him. Not just any old reward, not something simply nice to have, but a reward of such worth and importance that we would give up anything and everything we have to get it.

At its core faith has a very simple message which it embeds and repeats over and over to our soul: *God is Greater!* This is why people become willing to give up so much for His sake, from simply giving up of their time to gather regularly with other Christian's, to giving up money and possessions to love and bless others, to even being willing to give up their life rather than deny the truth about

God and His Son who died for us. Although there is so much more that can be said about faith, I believe this truly gets to the heart of the matter concerning what faith does in us, how it affects our character and motivates us.

## The Cloud of Witnesses

So, continuing in the book of Hebrews and taking what we've learnt about faith, about certainty and greatness; let's see it in action - what does it look like to be a person motivated by faith? And we'll start with Abraham: *"By faith Abraham obeyed when he was called to go out to a place that he was to receive as an inheritance. And he went out, not knowing where he was going"*[4]. By faith Abraham obeyed. How easy and simple to say, yet how hard such obedience would be without faith. He didn't even have the vigour of youth on his side, he was 75 years old by now. He couldn't call ahead first and book himself a piece of land to stay in, he didn't hang around and make detailed plans, checking websites about Canaan, but rather he gathered his household and servants with all they had, and went. Why? Because he took God at His word. God told him to go, and promised to bless him. Indeed God promised to bless him and make him a blessing ultimately to the whole world! That's quite a promise, and coming from anyone else would surely just be wind. Anyone could say those words, you probably hear politicians among others, regularly make high

---

4. Heb 11:8

minded and well-intended promises about things they simply don't have enough control over or power to do. Even our better leaders can leave us disappointed with the results compared to the promises. But Abraham packed up and left not knowing what he was going to find, or what he was going to face in this new land. He could be certain of nothing, except of the one sending him – he was certain of the ability and character of God. And that's what faith allows us to do too. It raises courage in us to step out when called by God, not knowing or being certain of all the details, but being certain of Him. *By faith Abraham obeyed.*

In turn, as God's promise to bless them started to take further shape, *"By faith Sarah herself received power to conceive, even when she was past the age, since she considered him faithful who had promised."*[5] Humanly speaking what was promised to Sarah – to give birth to a child at her age, was not just unlikely or improbable, it simply was not going to happen without God's power at work. But thank God, His promises and callings come not with a boot out the door and some encouraging words, but rather they come with power and with His presence. I love the way that Matthew's gospel ends; with the command and call to go and make disciples of all nations, *"And behold, I am with you always, to the end of the age."*[6] He doesn't say "now off you go, I'll see you at the end", but promises to be with them always. And we now know of course, that this promise was and is fulfilled through the receiving and the empowering of the Holy Spirit. God with, and in us!

5. Heb 11:11
6. Matt 28:20

For Sarah, her circumstances seemed to make it certain that she would never conceive, indeed to think otherwise was laughable. But Sarah became certain of God over the circumstances, and so Isaac was born. It was God who chose his name, which in a lovely touch on His part means 'he laughs'. Indeed after his birth, Sarah said "God has made laughter for me…"[7]

I've got a great quote stuck up on my wall at home, taken from an article[8] by Jon Bloom about feeling unqualified for what God is calling you to do. I turn to it whenever I start to feel the weight of what I'm called to and my laughable inadequacy to achieve it. These kinds of feelings are quite normal and arguably appropriate. But only if it's backed up by the faith that God Himself will do it through us. So, in turn, I'm also reminded to take stock when I'm feeling a bit too sure of own abilities, and to humble myself afresh as I see my own meagreness, alongside how bountifully greater God is. It can be an uncomfortable thing to depend on someone else, to let go and entrust things to others. But what a release and a glorious weight is lifted as our faith grows more and more to know with certainty that God rules and reigns above all, without limit in knowledge, wisdom or power. And what He has promised, He will do. So let's remember, It was *by faith Sarah received power* to achieve the promise made to her.

---

7. Gen 21:6
8. 'Don't feel qualified for your calling?', Jon Bloom, DesiringGod.org

## *The Trial of Time*

We should also consider another side to Abraham and Sarah's story, for though they are wonderful positive examples to us, the Bible is very honest about failures as well as triumph's in the lives of these witnesses. In Abraham and Sarah's case, the thing that weakened their faith is something that many, if not all followers of Jesus Christ have experienced – the trial of time. Or put another way, waiting for God to act. There were twenty-five years in total between God first promising to Abraham that he would have many descendants, being made into a great nation (and more), before the birth of Isaac. That is a LONG wait, and it's this trial of time that has undone so many people, with Abraham and Sarah being no exception. Imagine it, Abraham is already seventy-five years old when he gets this promise and Sarah sixty-six. They were already considered past it in terms of having children. But to grow twenty-five years older as they wait for the promise to be fulfilled must have been incredibly difficult. I often think that patience is one of those things that you think you have until it's actually tested. It perhaps would not have been so bad if they'd been told from the beginning that it would take that long. You'd at least have a date to look towards and hold on to in your heart. But perhaps that's why God doesn't often give dates and times – because He wants us to learn to hold on to Him rather than a date? So when we learn that partway through this period, their faith wavered and they tried to make the promise happen in their own strength, we can be more than a little understanding, whilst hopefully learning from it and not making the same type of mistake in our own lives.

It was ten years into this period that they decided to take matters into their own hands. Sarah suggested to Abraham that he should sleep with her Egyptian servant called Hagar. And it worked? Well, Hagar conceived and had a child named Ishmael. But the two women from then on had contempt for each other, and the peace they had sought through trying to make God's promise happen through their own means resulted in nothing but strife and division within the camp. It was not an act of faith, and so came with none of faith's benefits or fruits. *Thankfully God is also greater than our failures, and our faithlessness.* God blessed and looked after Ishmael, and Abraham and Sarah still lived to see the child of promise born, in His timing and His way.

### *Promises, promises...*

*"By faith Isaac invoked future blessings on Jacob and Esau"*[9] This is easily skipped over, indeed I had myself until someone pointed it out to me: he passed on or invoked future blessings. He passed on something he didn't physically have, just as Abraham had to him, and Jacob would to his sons – the promise that they would become a great nation and inhabit the land of Canaan. It would be a bit

9.  Heb 11:20

like me leaving in my will the promise of a million pounds to my children without actually having it (which I certainly do not), yet believing they would receive it. Madness? Wishful thinking? No, it was faith, because the person who had originally promised it is faithful. They had certainty that God was willing, able and eager to do it (in His timing). He had promised; therefore it would happen.

And don't all Christian parents want to be able to do this? To pass on their faith in the future blessings of being with Jesus Christ when He comes to reign once and for all time. When He makes a new heaven and earth which will never see sin! I know I do. I'm desperate that my girls will also receive this faith and the awesome future that comes with it. *By faith Isaac passed on future blessings.*

All of which leads us nicely onto our next example...


### Home

*"These all died in faith, not having received the things promised, but having seen them and greeted them from afar, and having acknowledged that they were strangers and exiles on the earth. For people who speak thus make it clear that they are seeking a homeland."*[10] The truth is that as Christians we've never even seen let alone been to our home. That moment you were born again, made new, you became a stranger to the world you knew and you became

10. Heb 11:13-14

an heir of the world to come. Do you feel that? Does the way you live reflect something of this truth? I know it's quite a challenge for myself. It's so easy to get caught up in investing in the here and now, and focusing only on what is in front of us. But it is a frequent trait found in those who are full of faith that their hearts are primarily set not on this life, but on the one to come.

We're sometimes told that 'home is where the heart is'. Well there's plenty of truth in that, and Jesus taught something very similar: that "…where your treasure is, there your heart will be also."[11] We need to ask ourselves what is it we treasure most? Because what we treasure and put our time, effort and money into shows where our hearts truly are. If our hearts are genuinely set on God and the future life we will have with Him - faces unveiled, seeing Him unhindered and full of joyful awe – then there will be evidence now in how we live that demonstrates this is what we treasure most.

Let's consider one type of example: As I write this I have two daughters, aged four and almost three. They have many, many things. So many toys, which mummy and daddy are largely glad to give, and their grandparents are all the happier to give them. From our position as parents we've got to a place of wanting to be careful how much they get and how quickly, because it's so easy to just get more and more, and stuff our lives with so many little (or big) things, without appreciating or valuing them. You just move on to wanting the next thing. What's much more concerning

11. Matt 6:21

(and annoying) about all this, is the realisation of how bad I can be, how easy it is for me to not appreciate what I have, and simply look to fill my own life with more stuff. I tell you, having children has been great for my walk with God thanks mostly to one key principle I've been trying to follow: Anything I get concerned or angry with my children about, I ask God in what way I do the same type of thing with Him. It's been wonderfully humbling.

Now I'm not about to say that having anything other than the very bare essentials is bad and 'un-Christian'. But we do well to remember how Jesus encouraged His hearers not to build up their treasures on earth where it won't last, but instead to build up your treasure in heaven where they will last forever. How seriously we take these words of His will be a good measure of how much we're truly looking forward to our true home with God. These great witnesses of the Bible showed that they were certain of a greater time and place to come. Not by sitting around and without any care for this life, no, they got on with it, but with a heart attitude of belonging to another place and time. Feeling like foreigners passing through till the promised land is finally reached. *"If they had been thinking of that land from which they had gone out, they would have had opportunity to return. But as it is, they desire a better country, that is, a heavenly one. Therefore God is not ashamed to be called their God, for he has prepared for them a city."*[12]

I'm finding more and more that as time goes on, I'm yearning for the day when I will never sin again. Oh, I'm

12. Heb 11:15-16

certain of Christ's sacrifice for me, that my debt is paid and I've been redeemed and saved from the punishment I deserved. I know I'm declared righteous before God because I am now *in* Christ who is truly righteous and holy. But in truth sin is still present in my life and I hate it. It brings me low and spoils to some level my relationship with everyone. Sin is a tiresome, enticing thing. But God has promised that when I'm raised again and given a new body I will be changed. Just as the power of sin over me was defeated at the cross, so the presence of sin in my life will be removed and finished with at Christ's return[13].

Now this longing in me, for my future sinless life with God is a comfort and encouragement to me, as it is, in itself, another sign of faith. These witnesses in Hebrews looked to and desired a better 'country' to come. But if they had wanted to, they would have been able to return to the land they'd come from. And it's the same with us, we are not forced to continue in a journey with God, we have the choice to return to the sins Christ died to save us from. It is a pitiful, lazy and poor choice to make, but one we are free to do. Oh, we all fail at times (daily – at least in my case), and each time it shows our imperfect faith. But praise God, Christ's blood remains more than enough to pay our debt of sin. Sadly, for some, sin remains too enticing and faith has not taken root in order to combat it and continually declare to their hearts that God is Greater! In the end, they do decide to return to 'the land' they had come from, abandoning Christ. Conversely, we're told that for those who want God,

---

13.  1 Cor 15:50-58

His ways and His ultimate plans, that God is not ashamed of them, not ashamed to be called their God. And has prepared a future life for them that will be better, that will be greater than they could even imagine.

Ask yourself honestly: where is home for you? What do you long for more? That which you find on this earth, or in the one to come? For if we're truly characterised and motivated by faith in God, it will affect our thinking and actions right here and now.

## Greater than death

Well, we're not finished with Abraham quite yet. The Bible tells us of another event that's hard to even imagine. *"By faith Abraham, when he was tested, offered up Isaac."*[14] God told Abraham to sacrifice his son, Isaac. Now you've got to remember that Abraham had no idea that God would stop him from doing it at the last moment. God had not yet revealed that He hates such practices[15], so there was no reason for him to think that he wouldn't have to go through with it. What was going through his mind as he led Isaac up that mountain? Well, the account in Genesis doesn't say, but Hebrews does: *"He considered that God was able even to raise him from the dead"*[16]. What faith! He considered, he reasoned, and came to the conclusion that the God who made the entire universe and who sustains all things, who had seen them through their troubles, who had always done

14. Heb 11:17
15. Lev 18:21
16. Heb 11:19

exactly as He said He would, who had promised that through Isaac, Abraham would have more descendants than grains of sand on the seashore – well then surely this same God will do something to make sure His promise is fulfilled. And he reasonably concluded that the only way God could do that is by bringing Isaac back to life. It's entirely logical. But only if you first understand who Abraham was dealing with. Knowing what He did about God, it was both reasoned and reasonable to go ahead and sacrifice his son believing that he would receive him back from the dead. *By faith Abraham, when he was tested, offered up Isaac.*

Before moving on, let's just take a moment to consider why God even did this. Why would God feel the need to test Abraham's faith? He's the God who knows the secrets and motivations of our hearts, who has known our every thought and action we'll ever make from before we were born. He already knows exactly what we'll do and why in every given situation. In Genesis we're told: "*He said, "Do not lay your hand on the boy or do anything to him, for now I know that you fear God.""*[17] In what way did God now know that Abraham feared Him, that He didn't before? In experience. And this episode in Abraham's life shows us that seeing in action, and experiencing our faith at work is important to God, beyond simply knowing that we would act in faith if challenged to. It also tells us that another outworking of faith will be a motivation to fear God.

---

17. Gen 22:12

## Worthy of greater fear

*"By faith Noah, being warned by God concerning events as yet unseen, in reverent fear constructed an ark for the saving of his household."* [18] The fear of God is one of those things that tends to be taken to extremes by the church as a whole. Where it's either overemphasised, and everyone is encouraged to do as they're told lest they be sent to hell, or in the other extreme, which seems more common in our age, there can be a distinct lack of any fear or reverence towards God. If it's overemphasised, often no time is given to the love and grace of God, that woos and encourages His people towards the better life He wants for them, picking us up when we fall. Nor indeed to the help He wants to give through the empowering of The Holy Spirit. Where it's under emphasised, people strive forwards to take seriously the good and nice promises of God in the Bible, but fail to take seriously and maybe even proactively ignore the warnings given by the same God in the same Bible.

We must for our own sake, cherish and hold up high both the kindness and severity of God as Paul puts it,[19] not simplifying our God and His character – a sad and dangerous thing to do. Faith can help us with this, as it did with Noah. There was no sense in Noah that God wouldn't actually wipe out the rest of humanity; no questioning how a God of love could do such a thing. He took God at His word and believed what He said. Both in terms of the coming judgement and what Noah needed to do save himself and his

18. Heb 11:7
19. Rom 11:22

family. It must have seemed crazy to those who knew him, spending who knows how long to construct a huge boat, far away from the sea in the belief that a flood, of indeed biblical proportions, was on its way from God! But he was carried along by faith, by certainty in the One who had warned him. Then in turn through a healthy, reverent fear of God. Noah knew to take God seriously when all those around him saw no reason to honour God at all.

Now don't go thinking that the God of the Old and New Testaments are different God's or that He's mellowed since the Old Testament times. He is the One and only true God, the same yesterday, today and forever. Unchanging in character or substance. That's why He's so dependable and unfalteringly true to His word and Himself. That's why we can trust Him entirely. We may now know and experience His love in ways that weren't fully revealed during Old Testament times, but remember, the way this is most fully expressed with Christ Jesus, His sacrificial death and glorious resurrection, was all planned from before the creation of the world. It's hinted at, foreshadowed and even foretold in so many ways in the Old Testament. The plan never changed, and God never changed.

So now, coming back the other way we must realise that the God we meet in the Old Testament is still the same God we encounter in the New Testament, not to mention in our daily lives now. The God of Noah, who justly judged the whole earth and decided to save a select few, is our very same God today. Remember all those people deserved to die in that way – God wasn't having a bad day, He was acting with complete justice, and one day He will judge the entire earth again. A day has been set when Christ will return to judge the living and the dead. This day will come – it's unavoidable, and is getting ever closer. The consequences of this judgement day will be utterly just, eternally lived with, and beyond our imagination - whether for the good or bad.

Now we have no ark to build, and no way to save ourselves. Instead, we have one provided: we're told that in repenting and believing in Christ and what He did for us, in being baptised in His name, we are now found *in Him* if we continue in our faith. Jesus Christ, He is our ark to save us from the wrath of God. We are now covered and credited with Christ's righteousness, His goodness, and furthermore have the Holy Spirit dwelling in us, changing us from the inside. God surrounding us, and God living inside us. Praise God that He's so incredibly thorough in His saving plan. And just like Noah, we'll have plenty of people mocking us for what we do and believe. They'll see no reason to prepare for a future judgement before the Lord of All. Noah could have given in to the sneering of others he must have experienced. After all, it's the easier thing to do. It would have taken a long time and a lot of effort to build the ark, plenty of time to question what on earth He was doing: was it really necessary or worth it? Will God truly do such a thing? But Noah didn't give in or hold back. He was carried along by a healthy, reverent fear of God, born in faith. And through this faith he saved both himself and his household.

Furthermore, Christ told His listeners: "do not fear those who kill the body but cannot kill the soul. Rather fear him who can destroy both soul and body in hell."[20] This is quite a stark statement that can't faithfully be softened. For some Christians around the world, this is sadly and immediately relevant – those whose lives are genuinely in danger because of their faith in Jesus Christ.

As it stands, though there are plenty who do have to stand up under these kinds of trials, many Christians aren't facing that kind of physical threat. But this teaching remains just as relevant, for if it applies to physical beatings, surely it must apply to verbal ones. How tempting it is to shrink back when we need to openly stand up for Christ, displaying our faith in Him through our words and actions. And all because we fear what others might say to us, or even simply about us. It's such a dishonour to God when we let fear get the better of us in this way, and shows a distinct lack of faith. This is not the outworking of a soul believing and continually discovering that God is greater in every way and over every circumstance. By shrinking back we're treating God as being of less worth than the people we're fearing. But good news - a faith born fear of God can release us from a fear of others. Far from being a bad thing, it is a blessing and a release, and personally, I desire to have more of it imbedded in my soul through faith in Him. *By faith Noah... in reverent fear constructed an ark for the saving of his household.*

---

20. Matt 10:28

## *The Golden Nugget*

Now we turn to the story of Shadrach, Meshach and Abednego, who are surely in mind when the author of Hebrews refers to those who *"quenched the power of fire."*[21] And it's here that we to return to the risk theme briefly mentioned earlier, in order to find that golden nugget of truth. Faith is not about risk. But it does provide a great foundation from which to take one. Shadrach, Meshach and Abednego (or Hananiah, Mishael and Azariah as they were originally known) were among the first group of Jews to be deported to Babylon. They along with Daniel were picked out to be trained as potential advisors to the king of Babylon - Nebuchadnezzar.

Through God's blessing and anointing on their lives they proved to be among the best, most helpful advisors he had. What could have been going through their heads? They endured so much change, having been captured and taken to an unfamiliar land, not knowing what to expect, and then ended up possibly in an even more privileged position than they'd had before in Judah? But this did not spare them from coming into conflict with a king who thought far too highly of himself. Nebuchadnezzar had a huge golden image of himself made, and I mean huge! The Bible records it as sixty cubits high, or in more modern measurements about twenty-seven meters. That's between three to four times higher than the height of the average house in the UK. Now when the music played everyone was required to bow down

---

21.  Heb 11:19

# FAITH 53

and worship the image. I like to imagine the king watching people walk along going about their daily lives and trying to order the music to start at awkward moments to catch people out. Almost like a game of musical chairs/bowing where the last one standing has to sit at the side and they move onto the next round? But disappointingly it wasn't like that at all, and to remain standing wasn't to lose a game but to lose your life. Nevertheless, these three men of faith remained standing. The result was to be brought before the king who gave them one last chance to bow before his golden image and worship it…

> *"Shadrach, Meshach and Abednego replied to him, "King Nebuchadnezzar, we do not need to defend ourselves before you in this matter. If we are thrown into the blazing furnace, the God we serve is able to deliver us from it, and he will deliver us from Your Majesty's hand. But even if he does not, we want you to know, Your Majesty, that we will not serve your gods or worship the image of gold you have set up."*

Dan 3:16-18

At first, it reads like they are absolutely certain that God will save them, and then they throw in a 'but': *"But even if he does not…"* They're not doing this because they know for sure God will save them (although they do seem fairly confident), but the point is they see God as worth dying for. Their faith, their certainty, is in a God both able to save, and who is worth surrendering their lives to, even if that means being burned alive. And so, from this rock-solid foundation, they are compelled to launch off and take the risk. I love how the whole thing comes across as being done in a calm, polite, matter-of-fact boldness.

Let's take another example of *faith-inspired* risk, featuring Jonathan (King Saul's son), and his armour bearer. I really like Jonathan's story. He seems to have been a genuinely good man and full of faith in God. It's a real shame his father wasn't more like him. Now on this particular occasion Jonathan and his armour bearer are out on their own and heading towards one of the Philistine's garrisons:

> *"Jonathan said to the young man who carried his armour, "Come, let us go over to the garrison of these uncircumcised. It may be that the LORD will work for us, for nothing can hinder the LORD from saving by many or by few."*

1 Sam 14:6

'It may be'. MAYBE! Again, we've got the solid foundation of faith: *"nothing can hinder the LORD from saving by many or by few"*, the certainty that their God is greater than the Philistines, which provides the launch pad from which to take a risk: *"It MAY BE that the LORD will work for us"*. That's quite a risk, two people up against a garrison of the enemy. We have no idea how many people were in that garrison, only that they killed about twenty in the first strike[22]. And it wasn't just Jonathan who was full of faith: *"...his armour-bearer said to him, "Do all that is in your heart. Do as you wish. Behold, I am with you heart and soul.""*[23] Really? I've got to admit my response may well have been more like: 'Well yes He *can* save with just the two of us, but wouldn't it be sensible to go and get a few (hundred) others?'

Both these stories have great outcomes and the hero's faith is rewarded straight away. But what if they hadn't? What if instead, we read of how Shadrach, Meshach and Abednego died in the flames refusing to bow down to the golden image, and of how Jonathan and his armour bearer died valiantly but needlessly attacking a garrison on their own? Would their stories be any less faith-filled? No of course not! Not so inspiring admittedly. But God loves to respond to faith because it pleases Him so much. And if not in this life, certainly in the life to come they would have received their reward. These stories, these lives, displayed something of God's worth, glory, and faithfulness, to all those who saw it happen.

So, remember faith is not about risk. But maybe, it might just motivate you to take the risk of your life, for the glory of God? Or perhaps more simply speaking up and taking the risk of being rejected or ridiculed for Jesus' sake? Because behind it all you have this certainty, this faith – that God is worth it. That He is greater.

---

22. 1 Sam 14:14
23. 1 Sam 14:7

## *Beyond the cloud*

*"And what more shall I say? For time would fail me to tell of..."*[24] So much could be said about each person and line written, but much like the writer of Hebrews did, I'm hitting a point where it feels right to move on. Beyond this great cloud of witnesses is the God-Man Himself. To follow their example our primary focus needs to be on Christ, not them. He's the one to set our sights on, and where our faith finds both its source and destination. He showed the way by doing what He did for the joy set before Him. Not duty, but joy. He too looked to the reward and found it greater.

Now we're encouraged to run our race, our life of faith, with endurance (we need to keep going, it's not going to be over quickly). And to do this well, we need to untangle ourselves from every "weight and sin"[25]. I don't care how good an athlete you might be, if you go into a race with a rope tied around you attached to stones, even if small stones, you're going to be held back from doing your best. And if they're too big you're going to be held back from moving at all!

Consider how faith in Christ changes how we relate to sin. No matter how badly you fell, or how deep you went into the abyss of sinfulness, Christ's sacrifice on the cross was greater, and His power over death was greater so that the grave could not hold Him down. As the earlier parts of the book of Hebrews tells us; Christ is a better mediator, a better High Priest of a better covenant, with a better

---

24. Heb 11:32
25. Heb 12:1

FAITH 57

message. He didn't just pay the penalty of our sins, He went beyond that, and now we who believe in Him have credited to our account His righteousness. You may have heard this helpful way of remembering what justification or being justified means. You break up the word to *Just As If I'd...* never sinned. But more than that, better than that, through Christ it's *Just As If I'd...* lived the perfect life of Christ. We go from having an unpayable debt, not to breaking even, but to being credited with something we could never earn. From God's enemies to God's adopted children. God's plan and means of salvation was and is so much greater than we could have ever dreamed up.

But there's more. In our on-going battle with sin in our lives, faiths internal whisper of encouragement – that He is greater, now starts to provide a more meaningful alternative in every situation, along with the power to follow it.[26] You see, so often, instead of simply trying harder when faced with any given temptation, what we need instead is to cultivate a superior desire – something even better to chase after. Jesus didn't come to give us a better rule book to live by, He came to bring freedom, to release us into fulness of life! So to address greed He says to His disciples, *"Do not lay up for yourselves treasures on earth, where moth and rust destroy and where thieves break in and steal, but lay up for yourselves treasures in heaven, where neither moth nor rust destroys and where thieves do not break in and steal."*[27] Reminding them also that this is a sign of where their heart truly is. Sadly there are far too many people both inside and

26. 1 Cor 10:13
27. Matt 6:19-21

outside the church who seem to think that following Christ is about denying yourself. And it is, but this is only half of the message! And a half-truth can be wholly false. We deny ourselves in order to go after what is better. The rewards of which may or may not be found directly in this life. In some ways, we'll discover the blessing of living as God wants us to right here and now, discovering that (wouldn't you know it), God really does know what He's talking about. And in some ways, we'll be like Abraham and the others on this list, who see the promise from afar, but will have to wait till Christ returns to receive the prize of our faith.

Another example of seeking this greater desire is found when Paul, briefly addressing drunkenness, encourages his readers to go on being filled with the Holy Spirit rather than filling themselves up on wine.[28] Now wine, of course, is not bad in and of itself, and Jesus Himself enjoyed it with His disciples. But so many have turned to wine and alcohol in its different forms to find escape from the mundane or grim parts of life. However, it is no saviour, and so often brings out the worst in people. The encouragement brought, is to seek to be filled with Him who empowers, brings love and fullness of life. Who brings out the very best in people.

Now it's not just the bad, but some good stuff can weigh us down too. God may well require of you to give up things perfectly fine in and of themselves, but that are getting in the way of your relationship with Him or the direction He has for you in life. I'll give you a couple of examples from my life. Firstly, games. I have at different

[28]. Eph 5:18

times become quite addicted to different games on my mobile phone. Things that started as just a helpful five-minute distraction or wind down from time to time, became all-consuming and started to occupy far too much of my time and thoughts. Several times over the years, God has spoken to me about putting a game down because of this. And each time I would, then months later I'd start on a new game. At first, all would be well, and it wouldn't consume me, indeed it would be a genuinely helpful occasional distraction. Then I'd start turning to it more and more till it occupied time that I might otherwise have spent speaking with God or thinking about His word. So for me, I've needed to put them down completely, as something that hinders more than helps me. Now there's nothing intrinsically wrong with playing games on your mobile, and for you, it's probably no issue at all? But if like me you know that it absorbs your time and mind more than is helpful, it's time to delete that game. Right now. You may not want to, but trust me it will do you good (as long as you don't fill that space in your life with something equally unhelpful. Been there. Done that).

Another example from my life concerns a hobby of mine. Like many people, I enjoy experimenting with food. I love to play with different flavours and methods, and come up with new dishes to enjoy with family and friends. I do this far less often now we have kids, but it's still something I find time to do, which I like to think I bless others with too (though they may just all be very polite). Not long ago I had an idea that would allow me to branch out into a completely new area: I had an inspiration for how I'd like to make and flavour my very own chocolate bar. I had discovered that they make small worktop chocolate refiners for people interested in giving it a go. It wasn't a completely silly price for me to consider, and I could probably save up for it over a year or two. However, praying one morning God simply told me to put the idea down, as it would be a distraction from what He has for me to do. Not that it was a bad thing, but rather a weight that would tangle me up and hinder me in my race at this time. So I did. It was a little disappointing of course, and I don't know the exact why, but it would be far worse not to listen to God's guidance and so miss out in other more important ways. Far worse still, would be to not listen and obey in this tiny little thing, where God spoke so clearly to me. I don't know about you, but if I find people aren't listening to me, I become less inclined to put much effort into speaking to them?

Whatever 'weight' it might be that God wants you to drop, it will require faith to do it. Once again, it's about that whisper being repeated from the core of your soul – "it's worth it because He is greater."

### *Help my unbelief!*

Perhaps the best news to discover amongst all this, is that God is also greater than our faith, or lack of. God does

FAITH   61

and always has started with us where we are, and continues with us every step of the way. Continuously moulding and shaping us like the master craftsman He is, giving us opportunity after opportunity to grow in faith. Jesus once met a man whose child was seized by an evil spirit. This spirit had made the boy mute and frequently caused him to convulse and foam at the mouth, which happened in Jesus' presence. It had been a problem since childhood and had sometimes cast the boy into either flames or water to try and kill him.[29] The disciples had been trying to cast the evil spirit out but without success. Then Jesus came on the scene, and the child's father turned to Him saying "*If you can do anything, please have compassion on us and help us.*"[30] If? Jesus didn't seem very impressed with this. If? Of course, I can, He says, anything is possible for one who believes! The response of this father was wonderfully honest and perhaps contained a little more faith than we give him credit for: "*I believe: help my unbelief!*"[31] And there, in a nutshell, we have one of our common problems: so often we're operating out of a mixture of faith and unbelief. There's so much going on inside us most of the time, some good, and some bad. But Jesus didn't turn away saying come back when you believe without any doubt. To be sure there were times when Jesus said he couldn't perform many miracles in a place because of their lack of faith[32]. And I don't think we should take that as being physically incapable. He could still do what He wanted as the all-powerful Son of God. But rather because He only did what

29. Mark 9:14-29
30. Mark 9:22
31. Mark 9:24
32. Matt 13:58

He saw His Father doing[33], what His Father wanted, and His Father wants to respond to and reward faith. And that's exactly what He did here. He responded to an imperfect but visible faith. Indeed, in the very words 'help my unbelief' the child's father was actually displaying some faith. It was right there in his appeal to Jesus for help. The father could see that there was reason to believe, but his weak and very human soul just wasn't fully there. He needed help, just like we all do at times, and he was asking just the right person. This small, weak, act of faith was enough because it still looked to God and honoured Him as the one capable of making the difference, the one who was greater than his unbelief.

In Matthew's Gospel, we're told of another detail about this event. After the boy had been released, the disciples asked Jesus why they were unable to cast out the evil spirit. This was a new experience for them. Jesus had already been sending them out in twos to heal the sick, cast out demons, teach repentance and about the kingdom of heaven.[34] Jesus responded to them saying *"Because of your little faith. For truly, I say to you, if you have faith like a grain of mustard seed, you will say to this mountain, 'Move from here to there,' and it will move, and nothing will be impossible for you."*[35] This has not tended to encourage me. My initial internal response to this is normally: 'If faith the size of a mustard seed can do that – just how small and pathetic is mine?!" It's a strong challenge, and one I shouldn't just brush aside. But maybe there's a bit more going on here as

33. John 5:19
34. Mark 6:7-13
35. Matt 17:20

well? There's another place in Matthew's gospel where Jesus uses the image of a mustard seed to describe the kingdom of heaven. Here He speaks of how this seed that starts off so tiny, grows into a tree larger than all the other plants in the garden.[36] So maybe alongside the challenge to my lack of faith, should also be the encouragement of potential? This seed of faith within me, that has already grown some, still has every possibility of growing into something much bigger and potent. And there's another thing to remember; as we considered at the beginning of the chapter, the primary and most important thing about faith is who or what you're putting it in. If our faith is in God, the Awesome Lord of All, who made the universe and all that's in it. Who loves to respond to people's faith in Him – well then even imagination can't limit what is possible through Him. As is so often the case, it comes back to a simple truth: We are weak, and He is strong. Thank God it's not primarily about us.

## Faith

So now we come to the end of this chapter on faith, and we ask: What does it look like to be a person characterised and motivated by faith? This person will know with certainty, at the core of their being, that God exists, that He is good, that He wants us to have a relationship with Him, and that He is worth pursuing above all else, because He is

---

36. Matt 13:31-32

quite simply greater. This will be displayed in every area of our lives, from our hidden thoughts to our words, and perhaps most strikingly our choices and actions. More and more we'll find that we're not hindered or motivated by fear of others or anything else, but that we're freed by a faith born fear of God, and a faith born desire for God. Where our every deed shows that we want and cherish God and His ways, more than anything and anyone else. Would you like this to be a good description of you? I know I would.

# ~5~

# Hope

Have you ever been through a hard time and had someone say to you "cheer up – it's all character building"? Were you blessed by this? No – me neither. Which is why its frankly annoying to discover that its really very biblical, and I don't even mean that the principle can be found as you bring various truths together – it's right there out in the open and plain to see in the book of Romans: *"Therefore, since we have been justified by faith, we have peace with God through our Lord Jesus Christ. Through him we have also obtained access by faith into this grace in which we stand, and we rejoice in hope of the glory of God. Not only that, but we rejoice in our sufferings, knowing that suffering produces endurance, and endurance produces character..."*[1]

Yes, you read it right, that utterly annoying (and probably somewhat wonderful) Christian friend of yours was correct! Almost. But this sentence from scripture wasn't over:

*"...Not only that, but we rejoice in our sufferings, knowing that suffering produces endurance, and endurance produces character, and character*

1. Rom 5:1-4

*produces hope, and hope does not put us to shame, because God's love has been poured into our hearts through the Holy Spirit who has been given to us."*

Rom 5:3-5

Hope. Why is it that no one encourages us to 'cheer up' or rejoice during harder times because of the hope it can ultimately produce? Why do we so often keep a step back and just go with the more general term: character? I think part of the reason is a self-feeding one, in that we simply neither talk about nor value hope properly. And when we do it's in general airy-fairy terms. We're told that the greatest of these is love.[2] We can infer that the foundation of these is faith. And sadly, in my view, the most neglected is hope.

In this chapter, we will be exploring the nature and purpose of hope, the second of the 'motivational characteristics', which God wants to embed in your soul, at the very core of who you are. In my experience hope is very rarely if ever taught about, whereas both faith and love are frequently talked about, and woven into other subjects. Maybe it's because hope is harder to pin down and talk about without coming across a little 'fluffy' and insubstantial? But the truth is without hope the soul withers, and in time gives birth to despair, which at its most extreme leads people to despair even of life itself. Hope is important!

---

2. 1 Cor 13:13

## *The expectation of future good*

Now just as it was with faith, we need to start by trying to define the hope we're talking about, as the way in which the word is most frequently used is not the biblical concept of hope. The main way that we tend to use the word hope is in an expression of optimism, such as: "I hope that the weather will be good this weekend". But it may or may not be accompanied by any expectation of this happening (especially if you live in the unpredictable north of England as I do). So you may hear precisely the same phrase from someone who has no real belief that it will turn out good. In this case, it's not even optimism but merely an expression of desire. It's a wish.

So what does the Bible say to help us understand? Well, just as we did with faith, we have to start with the simple and basic aspects, making sure we don't just rush over them because they seem too obvious. In doing so we find the truths which give us the right foundation needed to add more elements. Our main focus will be in Romans 5 where we started this chapter, but before we dive into that more deeply it will be helpful to skip ahead to something else the apostle Paul said in his letter to the Romans: *"...But hope that is seen is no hope at all. Who hopes for what they already have? But if we hope for what we do not yet have we wait for it patiently."*[3] Who hopes for what they already have? No one. The very nature of hope is to look to the future – to something we don't yet have, something good.

3. Rom 8:24-25 (NIV)

For we could also ask the question "who hopes for something bad to happen to them". No one. That is unless despair has taken over hope's role in someone's life, and even then, the bad they're wishing for is because they believe it will ultimately help them feel better. So we can define hope as *the Expectation of Future Good.*

It's a definition that will probably surprise few people, but it's helpful to actually pin down and say. These words have also been chosen carefully. Why 'expectation'? I've chosen to use this word as it allows for both certainty and vagueness, which as I'll try and show throughout this chapter is needed for a fully helpful definition of Hope. However, I must acknowledge straight away that I am treating this just slightly differently from anywhere else I've read about the original Greek. Pretty much everywhere I've read up about this has treated it as meaning an *assured* or *certain* expectation[4], making it more absolute and definitive than I'm doing. Now bear with me, and let me try to briefly run through why I think this isn't quite right. In the classical Greek of the time "elpis/elpizo" (hope) in Gentile use, was a personal projection of future events of all kinds, whether good or bad, but there was no certainty attached to it. Depending on the context, the word might have been used to describe fear instead of hope. So for many, the word meant something much broader and more subjective than how we tend to use the word. But for the Jews, because of the translation into Greek of their Hebrew scriptures, they were used to the word always being used positively, denoting

---

4. One example is: The NIV Theological Dictionary of New Testament Words, edited by Verlyn D. Verbrugge, Zondervan, 2000

confidence and trust (in God). So as we hit the New Testament we have people writing to others who are used to the word being used in a variety of ways, with a mixture of Jewish and Gentile believers. Now it's here in the New Testament that the claim is made that 'hope' is always used of an assured expectation, and I would indeed agree that the hopes spoken of are indeed absolutely certain – usually. But not always. There are several places where to my mind it seems to be used in a looser way, such as Paul's expectation (not absolute certainty) of coming to visit the Corinthians:

> *"For I do not want to see you now just in passing. I hope to spend some time with you, if the Lord permits."*
>
> 1 Cor 16:7

Also, saying that most hopes spoken of in the Bible are a certainty, is not quite the same thing as saying that hope itself carries or embodies the meaning of certainty. To my mind treating it this way becomes less helpful when considering hope's function more broadly.

Consider this from Hebrews:

> *"So when God desired to show more convincingly to the heirs of the promise the unchangeable character of his purpose, he guaranteed it with an oath, so that by two unchangeable things, in which it is impossible for God to lie, we who have fled for refuge might have strong encouragement to hold*

> *fast to the hope set before us. We have this as a sure and steadfast anchor of the soul, a hope that enters into the inner place behind the curtain, where Jesus has gone as a forerunner on our behalf, having become a high priest forever after the order of Melchizedek."*

> Heb 6:17-20

Hope is an anchor for the soul, to keep us steady in turbulent times. But anchors don't always work, they can fail if not used properly or if the water is simply too deep. What makes this anchor so sure? What makes it unbreakable and long enough for any situation? It's God Himself. It's His perfect and unchanging character, it's His inability to lie, make a mistake, be surprised, or come up against a force even close to being greater than He is. If God has promised, then that is that, you can be absolutely sure of it, because you can be absolutely sure of Him.

Consider where we started in Hebrews looking at faith: *"faith is the assurance of things hoped for, the conviction of things not seen"*[5]. Faith is about certainty, but to consider hope in the same way makes this sentence a little redundant: "faith is the assurance of things you're certain of...". If you're certain about something you don't need assurance of it. You're either certain or you're not. And whilst we're here let's notice one more thing; it looks like the writer here is saying the same thing in two different ways to emphasise the point: assurance of hope, and conviction of things unseen. Assurance and conviction, hope and the unseen. So

---

5. Heb 11:1

it affirms our earlier point that you don't hope for what you already have, but something that you don't – something unseen. Also, it starts to hint at part of the way hope affects and motivates us – hope is linked to our sight or the way we view life, something we'll explore throughout this chapter.

So hope's source and centre is where the certainty is; our unchanging God, what He's like and what He's said; Christ Jesus, what He's done, doing, and will yet do at His return. But hope's intended flow and function in our lives is both broader and vaguer than to label it as merely another word for certainty. Whereas faith is all about certainty, Christian hope stands on certainty, or to continue the sailing theme from before; hope's anchor is firmly sunk into the bedrock of an unchanging and awesome God. It's a subtle difference at first glance, but if we don't make the distinction we end up with faith by another name. And whilst our faith is amazing and irreplaceable, equally, we don't want faith to replace one of God's other gifts to us. Hope's function is more varied and life-giving than to simply be a comforter or a steadfast anchor during life's storms. Hope keeps us holding on and looking forward in the bad times, and keeps us looking up and moving forward in the good times, filling us with joyous anticipation.

## *Working on the production line*

We return now to the part of Romans where we started this chapter, and Paul is getting excited. By now he has taken his readers through some hard-hitting truths about our nature and predicament before a just and righteous God, and in turn the incredible grace He has given to us through faith in Christ Jesus – making us right before God without compromising His justice. Building on this Paul now says because of this grace in which we now stand *"we rejoice in hope of the glory of God"*[6]. We look forward to the day when we'll see the glory of God, face to face – when we'll know God fully just as we are fully known to Him[7]. How incredible will that be! But *"not only that"*, he says, *"we rejoice in our sufferings"*[8]. What?! Why on earth would we rejoice in our sufferings? Well Paul moves straight into explaining; *suffering produces endurance* – ok, I can see that, the old 'whatever doesn't kill you makes you stronger' type thing and you start to find that you can cope more? Then; e*ndurance produces character* – well yes, I guess I can say that I can see in my own life and others how enduring times of suffering has strengthened and built up character. And finally; *character produces hope.* Now, this last step isn't as immediately obvious as the others, but I believe the reason is this – our growth and building up in character is evidence of God's sanctifying work in us.

We've already briefly considered in this book how God desires that we engage with Him in growing more and more

6. Rom 5:2
7. 1 Cor 13:12
8. Rom 5:3

# HOPE 73

into the people He made us to be. To live fuller, more rewarding lives, through His Spirit's work within us. And so this evidence of God working these hard and difficult times into something of great worth – better character, in turn, produces hope, because we have the evidence right there in us of God with us, and at work bringing good fruit out of bad times. All of this serves to strengthen our foundation from which we expect God to do more good things in the future.

But please note – this process is not automatic. This production line which starts with suffering doesn't inevitably lead to hope. Indeed, not everyone comes out the other side better. Whereas some come through maybe more determined or caring; mentally stronger or sympathetic, others come out bitter or hating; arrogant or self-seeking. Others still, come out entirely unchanged in terms of character. I wonder if the key doesn't lie in something we looked at in Chapter 3 of this book from Hebrews:

> *"For the moment all discipline seems painful rather than pleasant, but later it yields the peaceful fruit of righteousness to those who have been trained by it."*

Hebrews 12:11

Notice here that the discipline from God, only results in good fruit for those who have been trained by it. I'm certain that God is working all sorts of stuff into our lives and characters without us realising it straight away, but once again there is an expectation on us to engage with what God is doing. The *out*-working of faith, hope and love, when they're already embedded in the core of our being, is an automatic and wonderful one – if they're there it'll just ooze out of you to some level without you even trying. However, the *working in* of these things takes time. It will require a more conscious surrender and working alongside God in His plans to see them established. So now when I'm in the midst of more difficult periods, I'm trying to remember to ask God what it is that He wants to work into me through them? How is He trying to help me grow and develop, what good can be forged in this bad? (Alongside pleading that He'll get me out the other side quickly).

So when you're traveling through a darker time in life, take heart. For God will see you through to better times, whether in this life or the next. And if you're open to being trained by it, God will build up in you hope, a precious gift of more worth than words can describe.

### The old familiar rod

Thankfully, God is a God of many means and methods, and suffering is not the only tool He uses to build up hope in our souls. As Paul says later in this same letter:

*"For whatever was written in former days was written for our instruction, that through endurance*

*and through the encouragement of the Scriptures we might have hope."*

Romans 15:4

Reading through God's interactions with His people recorded in the Bible has such potential to give us hope. So many different and flawed characters, just like us, for whom God stepped in and made the difference. We read and begin to understand How God deals with us, and His plans to release us from bondage to sin, so that instead we may be bound to Him. It's glorious, strengthening, hope enhancing stuff. But again, the process is not automatic. It is entirely possible to study the Bible hard, learn the background to all the different books within it, memorise vast portions, and yet have no real relationship with God. This is because it's not being treated as the all-authoritative word of God, and so sadly it doesn't build us up as it could. The Bible will not have its due impact on us if we don't come to it in faith that it is from God, and that He knows better than we do. We must come open and surrendered, doing our very best not to put our views on it, but instead letting it align our views with His. When we do, we're opening ourselves up to have this hope grown, encouraged and watered within us – along with many other good things.

Now the problem with talking about this is that it can feel like the old familiar rod coming back out to beat us up again, knowing as we do, that we should probably pray and read the Bible more. Isn't that the lesson we so often hear?

And we've heard it so many times, that we tend to feel both guilty and numbed by the challenge. I hate thinking about how much of my life I've spent not being disciplined enough to make sure I set aside this sort of regular time with God. And then I move on from thinking about it because so much is going on which needs my attention. Or perhaps I simply feel the need to flop and do nothing for a bit, because I'm already so tired from everything else. Why is it, that bad habits are so easy to form, but hard to stop; whilst good habits are hard to form and easy to stop?

As I said - the rod is hard to avoid when talking about this, and though many of us are already numb to it, if we're honest, we know full well that we need a bit of a prod to get us on track. But let me attempt to bring out both the 'carrot and the stick'. You probably know well the story of Mary and Martha. Jesus entering a village is welcomed by Martha into her home, where Jesus starts talking and teaching many things. Mary sits with the others listening, whilst her sister is busy getting food ready for everyone on her own – getting all the jobs done, whilst silently getting more and more annoyed with Mary for not helping. That is until she stops being silent and says: *"Lord, doesn't it bother you that my sister has left me to do all the work by myself? Tell her to come and help me!"*[9] But Jesus doesn't. As is so often the case He turns it around, and with care pouring out, gently challenges Martha *"…You are worried and upset about many things, but only one thing is necessary. Mary has chosen what is best, and it will not be taken away from*

---

9. Luke 10:40

*her*."[10] How difficult it is to judge this right. Because there are many things that we genuinely need to get done, and God would also admonish those who too easily let their responsibilities slide. But we can't just dismiss the challenge claiming that we simply have too much to do. That would be to ignore part of God's word by making excuses for ourselves. If we don't have time, then we're doing too much, and it's something else that should be let go of or reduced. If we can't 'fit God in' to our lives, then something is very wrong. Indeed, if we come at it with the mindset of simply trying to fit Him and His word in, then we're already coming at it with the wrong attitude.

There are two sentences I keep before me to challenge and encourage me in this area. The first is a book title: *'Too Busy Not To Pray'*. I confess I've never read the book. Simply reading its title I get challenged and feel like nothing more needs to be said. It remains on my bookshelf as a reminder to not *make excuses*, but instead to *make time* for prayer, especially when I'm busy. The other sentence I referred to in chapter 1: *'Feeding Leftovers To A Hungry God'*. Wow does that pierce my heart at times. It's so easy to just fit God in around other things and give Him just the scraps of our day, or even week or month. Quite simply, if the way we arrange our days suggest that God is an add-on, a blessed extra when we can fit Him in, instead of the highest priority of our minds, then something is seriously wrong!

---

10. Luke 10:41-42

It can be really hard to get this right, and once you've got it right, somewhere down the road, you might have to change it to keep it right? As a wise man once said to me, *"you'll find that you need to keep re-learning the same lessons"*. And this is partly because circumstances change. This might be through getting married, having kids, changing jobs, or simply because your own physical or mental capabilities alter over time (for the better or worse). It might be that at one time, spending time with God late in the evening worked great for you, and you were alert and had good times. But slowly you've started to find that you're less switched on as it gets later in the day, so you need to either alter your routine or find new ways of making the most of that time.

In these things, we must support and help each other, and it's worth asking yourself the question: "Can I be a Martha for a Mary sometimes?" My wife and I do this most weekends. We both give the other one some time to spend alone with God, whilst the other person does jobs and looks after the children. This has been a good and helpful step forwards for us, as we've adjusted to the major life change of having two children added into our family.

## *Carrot hunting*

Well, that's quite enough of the 'stick' for now, and this is not a book about getting our personal time with God sorted out. So let's briefly consider what 'carrots' are there to feast on. And it's quite simple really – it will do you good. I mean such incredible good! And you'll need to maintain it to truly know its ongoing benefits. But simply put, God has given us His Word, and granted us access into His presence, any place, any time, in order to bless us. We're missing out when we don't make time and prioritise Him in this way – and surely we don't want to miss out on such a great thing. I find the saying we take from the Bible that: *"the spirit indeed is willing, but the flesh is weak"*[11] to be all too true in me, especially in this kind of context (indeed the original context is about the disciples failing to stay up and pray with Jesus). A part of me really wants to, and the other part is always trying to get out of it because it feels like too much effort. But whenever I win that battle, I'm always so pleased that I bothered to try and push through, and I can feel its worth. What's more, the busier I am, the greater my need for it, and so the more potential it has to prove itself fulfilling, and worth fighting for.

Why do it? Because God blesses us through it, and among other things, will use it to build us up in life-giving, God-exalting hope. That's a pretty good carrot.

---

11. Matt 26:41

## *Finding foundations*

We return now to our passage in Romans, where Paul continues: "and hope does not put us to shame, because God's love has been poured into our hearts through the Holy Spirit who has been given to us."[12] Why would hope put us to shame? It would put us to shame if it failed us. Indeed, if we put our hope in God, and in the end, He was unable or unwilling to do all that He had promised, other people would have good reason to mock and shame us. Maybe this is partly why we find some Christians hesitant to hope for good things. You hear phrases such as 'I dare not hope' because they don't want to risk being disappointed. Solomon in the book of Proverbs counselled his readers that "Hope deferred makes the heart sick"[13]. I know what he means, I doubt that there is anyone who hasn't experienced this; having your expectations raised so high, with your heart open and ready to receive what you've desired for so long. Then it doesn't happen. It gets delayed again, and again, and you get to a stage where you don't want to hope anymore because of the pain it's caused you.

Let me say right now that God wants you to have hope. To know this great and uplifting gift, and to let it play a key role in defining you. Hope may be more than mere optimism, but that's not to say that it doesn't have that kind of effect in you. God wants to free you from the pessimism that so easily invades and drags us down. More than that – pessimism makes a comfortable couch for us to sit in and

12. Rom 5:5
13. Proverbs 13:12

safely moan from. It's this comfort factor that in part makes it so hard to break free from. The other main factor is this fear that in turn we wrap around ourselves like a warm blanket, whilst sat in a dull self-confined space. It can be so incredibly hard to motivate yourself to break free from this situation. These self-made chains can feel so snuggly, but chains they certainly are. This is not the fullness of life that God has called you to, or that Christ died to give you.

So how do we nurture a hope that brings life to our fragile souls, and neither makes our hearts sick or leads us to feel shame. Well, this is another one of the great works of the Holy Spirit – something that He delights to do in us. The Spirit is responsible for bringing about the Bible as we have it. He has worked through many different people with different personalities and situations, over many, many years. With gleeful pleasure, He takes the truths contained within it and makes them alive and active in our minds. And so, to establish this hope securely, God pours His love into our hearts through the Holy Spirit, by making the truth of what Christ has done for us ring with such incredible, overwhelming love. You see at just the right time; Christ died for the ungodly – that's you and me. And therefore, He did it when we were His enemies. It's rare enough for someone to die for a friend, but to purposefully die to save your enemies is something else entirely.[14] How much more can we depend on the love of God now we're 'in Christ', adopted into God's family and treated as co-heirs with Jesus Himself.[15] Or as Paul puts it; "how much more, now that we

14. Rom 5:6-8
15. Rom 8:15-17

are reconciled, shall we be saved by his life".[16] And again; "He who did not spare His own Son but gave Him up for us all, how will He not also with Him graciously give us all things?"[17]. What is there now that can separate you from the love of God? Can trials, distress, persecution, famine, nakedness, danger, or the sword? Of course not[18]. So whatever your situation you can be sure of your loving position before God. He gave the greatest gift to you as an enemy, so you can be sure He's not going to abandon you now He's made you family. You have every reason to have hope in God.

This is not to say that you should expect every aspect of life to go smoothly and that from now on everything is going to go your way because God loves you. There has been far too much teaching along those lines in different places, and it can only lead to disappointment, disillusionment, despair, or even denial. Because it's simply not true and is not what the Bible teaches at all. Amongst all these encouragements about God's love, there is also plenty of talk about suffering in different forms. And notice that it doesn't say that God's love will separate and keep you from trials, distress, persecution, famine, nakedness, danger and the sword. But rather that these things won't separate you from His love. He won't abandon you in them, and their presence doesn't mean He doesn't love you anymore. Indeed, it may be more that you've been counted worthy to endure them for His sake?[19] Which is utterly

---

16. Rom 5:10
17. Rom 8:32
18. Rom 8:35
19. Acts 5:41, 2 Thes 1:4-5

amazing, but sadly not the way that most of us tend to look at it.

## *Little words*

Sometimes it's the little words that carry such importance, and it's worth taking a moment to note the difference between hoping *for*, and hoping *in*. As Christians, we put our hope *in* God. As we've already considered; God is unchanging, and totalling dependable. He is all-powerful and all-knowing, so can't be overcome by force or the intelligence of another person. He is also of perfect character, and will never lie, go back on His word or be unfaithful in any way. He has a love for us so strong, that He gave His greatest gift to us whilst we were still His enemies, and through His only Son made us who believe in Him into His family through adoption. Therefore, our hope *in* God is utterly, unbreakably secure. There will always be a reason to have hope because there is always God. Even if we came to a place where all is lost and we face a hideous death, we know that God Himself awaits us on the other side. Death is not the end for a Christian. Or rather, death is only the end of all that was bad. We know we'll be resurrected with new bodies, like Christ's new body[20] no longer with any entanglement to sin, or fear of facing death again. Finally, fully, free. This is where we have certainty.

Now, what we hope *for* often doesn't carry such certainty. We may hope for God to remove an illness or

20. Php 3:20-21

obstacle from our lives. Or on a more positive note, that God will help us get that job, achieve that goal, win that competition. And there are so many great examples and testimonies of what God has done in people's lives. Many healed, impossible situations turned on their heads, forgiveness being found and love shared between former enemies. The financial means found in unexpected ways to achieve goals and help others. But there are also many examples of things not going to plan, of hopes painfully ended. So often what we hope *for* eludes us, maybe just for a while, maybe for many, many years, or perhaps it will never be. It was never wrong to hope *for* these things; the problem only arises when we place our hope *in* them. When we do this, we're making it so that our hope, our expectation of future good, is dependent on that thing or that person. So for example, you may have been desperate for a certain someone to ask you out, or for them to say yes if you ask them out. If this goes wrong, it's heart-breaking regardless. But if all your hope was *in* a possible relationship with that person, instead of hoping *for* that relationship, your loss is even greater. As far as you can see that's it, and the whole world has ended as far as you're concerned! If you haven't experienced this, you've most likely at least seen it happen with others? Their life is of course not over, it just seems like it from their perspective, and time will show them otherwise.

God wants you to expect good things to happen, you're His child and He loves you dearly. But like any good parent that doesn't mean He'll give you whatever you want whenever you want it. There are so many things at play that we simply don't yet understand, and will not in this life. By placing our hope *in* Him, whenever things go wrong and what we hope *for* doesn't come to pass, we'll find that this God-centred hope at the core of our souls is undented and undiminished, because its source has not changed or weakened. God is still the same awesome God, who works all things, no matter how painful or difficult to bear, for the ultimate good of those who know and love Him.[21]

## *Hope's function*

It's funny in a way, suffering leads to hope, and it's hope that plays such a big role in helping us through suffering. Hope toughens you up for trials and enables trials to toughen you up. But we're doing ourselves a disservice if we only regard it as something to help us when things aren't going well. If that was its only role, then it wouldn't be relevant in the life to come where there will be no more pain and suffering. So what does hope actually do? For a start, it helps us feel both lighter and stronger. It lifts our sights and our spirits, whilst also strengthening our souls and determination. It keeps us holding on and looking forward in the bad times, and keeps us looking up and moving forward in the good times. God wants a people who are expecting to

---

21. Rom 8:28

see Him do good and great things, and hope is His great gift to embed this attitude in us.

Love, we're told is the greatest of these. I believe we can, in turn, say that Faith, is the foundation of these. And perhaps the best description we can give here, is to say that Hope, is the lifter of these. Hope lifts our sight to God, to remember what He's done, see what He is like, and remember what He has promised. In turn, this frees our souls to soar! Hope lifts them up to see a view beyond the troubles, to see an end to pain and a God who is able to rescue and make all things work for good. Hope lifts our strength and resolve, enables us to stand and stay faithful to our faithful God no matter what happens in this life. Hope lifts our sights to dream great dreams, and strive forwards exploring new things God has for us instead of just finding a comfortable spot to stay. It lifts us up not just to endure hard times, but to keep moving and pursuing God in the good times. Hope is a wonderful and often undervalued gift of God. We need to learn to cherish and cultivate it.

## *Fear can hold you prisoner*

You may have seen what is now a fairly old film: The Shawshank Redemption? I along with many others love this film. It's a real shame that there's so much bad language in it, certainly in the early parts of the film, but it's worth pushing through with, and I know no better film about hope.

The film brilliantly depicts the difference hope can make in someone's life, or indeed its absence. There's a tag line never used in the film, but that appeared on the posters: "*Fear can hold you prisoner; Hope can set you free.*" There's a lot of truth in that, and although it's probably faith that's the biggest weapon against fear, it's hope that is fear's opposite. For surely a good definition of fear is: 'the expectation of future bad'?

So as we draw this chapter to a close, let's consider two sad stories where fear held people back, held them captive and caused them to miss out on what God had for them. In this, we will see the contrast of being motivated by fear or by hope. Indeed, in these two cases, we should actually say faith and hope, for rarely are any of our core three motivators operating on their own.

## *The Promised Land*

Our first story is from the Old Testament, the Israelites have been rescued from slavery in Egypt, and have been spending time getting to know God and His requirements of them. The law has been given, the Levitical Priesthood established, and all this while God has been miraculously providing for their needs; manna from heaven, water from rocks, battles won, and even the simple fact that neither their clothes nor their sandals have worn out during this time (and neither will they until they're in the promised land)[22]. Now

22. Deut 29:5

they're finally preparing to enter and conquer the promised land, so on the Lord's command spies are sent, twelve in total, and after forty days they returned with their report:

*"We came to the land to which you sent us. It flows with milk and honey, and this is its fruit. However, the people who dwell in the land are strong, and the cities are fortified and very large...We are not able to go up against the people, for they are stronger than we are."* So they brought to the people of Israel a bad report of the land that they had spied out, saying, *"The land, through which we have gone to spy it out, is a land that devours its inhabitants, and all the people that we saw in it are of great height."*[23]

They saw two things very clearly; first, that the land was as good as promised – there was no hype, God was as good as His word and it does indeed flow with milk and honey, a beautiful and fertile land. Secondly, they saw that the opposition were strong, very strong. With large fortified cities, and indeed large fort-like people, giants. They would later go on to compare themselves as being grasshoppers in comparison. But don't let this obvious exaggeration deceive you – the people in the land were strong, indeed *some* may have even been 'giants', even if nowhere near as big as they suggested (think more along the lines of Goliath who was around nine feet, or a little under three metres!). But they failed to see one thing. God.

It is unwise to go into a situation without knowing what you're facing – both the rewards and the challenges. But how much more foolish is it when we don't trust God and

---

23. Num 13:27-28;31-32

take Him at His word. By now, God had repeatedly revealed His power, His ability to sustain and to look after the Israelites, and the spies had now seen with their own eyes that God does not exaggerate (He is always true) – the land was as good as He had promised. But this is not where their eyes held their focus, and so fear took the place of faith and hope. The result? Infection. A whole nation was persuaded by the fear of ten spies, that the job of conquering the land was too hard and could not be done. They rebelled against God and would have stoned Moses along with the few people who stood by him in this matter, had God not intervened[24]. His response is a sobering one. At first, He threatens to wipe out the people and start again building a nation out of Moses and his descendants. But Moses intercedes, and pleading for God's own namesake among the other nations[25], God agrees to spare the people (don't ever think that prayer doesn't really make a difference). Nonetheless, there are still consequences: *"The LORD replied, "I have forgiven them, as you asked. Nevertheless, as surely as I live and as surely as the glory of the LORD fills the whole earth, not one of the men who saw my glory and the miraculous signs I performed in Egypt and in the desert but who disobeyed me and tested me ten times - not one of them will ever see the land I promised on oath to their forefathers. No one who has treated me with contempt will ever see it."*[26]

Sobering. Forgiveness is sought and found for the people, but fear has held them back from following God and

24. Num 14:10
25. Num 14:11-19
26. Num 14:20-23 NIV

entering the land He promised to them. Fear has led them to treat God with contempt, and so they'll live out the rest of their lives in a wilderness. Fear can indeed hold you prisoner.

### *Gerasenes*

Our next sad story is found in the New Testament, just after Jesus calms a storm by simply commanding it. He and His disciples have now sailed from Galilee to the other side of the lake to the country of the Gerasenes. There near the shore, Jesus encounters a man who had long been plagued by a 'Legion' of demons. At times this man had been kept under guard by the locals, chained and shackled, but he would break his bonds and be driven by the demons into the desert to live naked among the tombs. But this is not the saddest bit of the story. Upon seeing Jesus, the demons within the man know their time is up, and curiously ask to be sent into a nearby herd of pigs. Equally curiously Jesus allows this, and the demons leave the man, enter the pigs, causing them all to go rushing down into the lake and drown. A dramatic event to be sure, which is witnessed by the pig's herdsmen who go and tell the nearby city. Now, this is where we hit the truly sad part: "*...and the people went out to see what had happened. When they came to Jesus, they found the man from whom the demons had gone out, sitting at Jesus' feet, dressed and in his right mind; and* *they were afraid. Those who had seen it told the people how the demon-possessed man had been cured. Then all the people of the region of the Gerasenes asked Jesus to leave them, because they were overcome with fear. So he got into the boat and left."*[27].

This story kind of breaks my heart. In the last one we see fear taking hold because the people *couldn't* see that God was with them, and the complete difference He makes to a situation. In this story, fear took hold of them because they *could* see God at work and the difference He was already making. Once again, instead of faith and hope rising in their hearts, fear took their rightful/helpful place, and they asked Him to leave. So He did. No fuss, no trying to argue or reason with them. They had been visited by the God-man, Jesus Christ, who had done a wonderful work and set a man free from a horror I can barely begin to appreciate. Why? Why did this give birth to fear? We can be so easily afraid of change and the unknown, the powerful and uncontrollable. Jesus represented all these things to them immediately. He'd only just arrived, but already He's changed and rescued a man they could not help or tame. He'd shown great authority, speaking to and commanding demons to leave, and they obeyed, for they had no choice. Jesus was obviously like no man they had ever encountered before, and they simply did not know what to make of Him.

When God is at work, it can sometimes get a little scary. Out of the ordinary things can happen, and even though they're wonderful acts to bless people in different

27. Luke 8:35-37 NIV

ways, they can make you feel very vulnerable and out of control. Indeed, you're *not* fully in control. In turn, you can let fear put up a shield around you to "protect" yourself from what's going on, and sure enough, God will pass you by. But some time later you will find that it was no shield, but rather a cage of your own making, which prevented you from stepping into all that God wants to give and do in/through you. Fear can hold you prisoner.

There's another possibility. Maybe it was about the cost? They had just lost around two thousand pigs![28] That would be a lot to lose now, I presume it would be much more significant in those days. So Christ's presence had already cost them substantially – what might be the price if He stayed? Following Christ will always involve cost, and you should have no doubts and no surprises about this. Jesus was quite clear: *"Whoever does not bear his own cross and come after me cannot be my disciple. For which of you, desiring to build a tower, does not first sit down and count the cost, whether he has enough to complete it? Otherwise, when he has laid a foundation and is not able to finish, all who see it begin to mock him, saying, 'This man began to build and was not able to finish'… therefore, any one of you who does not renounce all that he has cannot be my disciple."*[29]

What does it cost to follow Christ? Everything. That is to say, you must surrender everything to Him, your whole life and all that you have. You may or may not be called upon to actually give it all up, but our attitude must be at a

28. Mark 5:13
29. Luke 14:27-30;33

place where we're ready and willing to. To believe and follow Christ Jesus means to fully submit to Him. *"You are not your own, for you were bought with a price"*[30]. Such a cost, such a surrender, can be a scary thing, and it's easy to see how fear could find a way in here. But as a friend of mine likes to say: "You can't out-give God." And he's right. Whatever God asks or demands of us is for our good. There is nothing given to God (if given rightly) that won't be paid back many times over. Not because He is then in your debt, far from it - we owe everything to Him eternally, but because He delights to do this. As John Ortberg In his book 'The Me I Want To Be' says:

> *"On the other side of death is freedom, and no one is more free than a dead man. Jesus had much to say about death to self, and on the journey to the me you want to be, you'll have some dying to do. But that kind of death is always death to a lesser self, a false self, so that a better and nobler self can come to life."*[31]

So let us do the math and count the cost. What is this cost? Everything, our very lives included. What's the reward? More. Knowing and being with God Himself, and fullness of life in ways we cannot imagine (but that shouldn't stop us trying). If you let fear shackle you and hold you back from surrendering anything or everything to Christ, you will lose out. Fear will hold you prisoner, and in turn rob you blind.

30. 1 Cor 6:19-20
31. John Ortberg, The Me I Want To Be, P26, 2010

## *Hope can set you free*

As sad as these two stories are, they aren't without the seeds of hope either. Forty years later the Israelites would return, with the old generation who treated God with contempt having all passed away. Just two remained Joshua, and Caleb, the only spies who came back having seen exactly the same things, but who also saw God for who He is. They had remained faithful and tried but failed to persuade the others that they could conquer the promised land because God was with them. It must have been a frustrating forty years waiting, but their hope did not diminish and return they did. This time with a new generation, with eyes of faith and hope, ready to follow God and claim His promise to them. As for the man freed from demons at Gerasenes – he wanted to leave that place with Jesus. But Jesus told him to return home and declare all that God had done for him. Which he did, throughout the whole city.[32] Who but God knows what ground-work that man did in preparing the people of that city to hear the gospel of Jesus Christ; His life, death and resurrection? A seed was planted there that day, and I'm sure God made it grow and bear fruit.

Is there any area of your life where fear is holding you back?

- Fear will focus on the fact that you could be hurt. Hope will remind you that Jesus suffered in so many,

[32]. Luke 8:38-39

and such extreme ways. And that even if you are hurt, you have a God of peace and comfort, who is worth hurting for.
- Fear will focus on the potential pain of rejection. Hope will remind you that Jesus was rejected, even by those closest to Him. But He will never abandon you.
- Fear tells you that you're not good enough, that it could go horribly wrong, and you will look like a fool. Hope will remind you that God loves you and accepts you before you even begin. That He will be with you, and that we could never do it without Him anyway.
- Fear will focus on the potential of failing. Hope will remind you how God works good through all things including your failures.

And of course, hope lets you see that anything could go far better than you can even imagine. It frees you not just to know that God can do wonderful things, but more than this – with anticipation, to *expect* God to do good and great things. *Fear can hold you prisoner; Hope will set you free.*

*"May the God of hope fill you with all joy and peace in believing, so that by the power of the Holy Spirit you may abound in hope."*

Romans 15:13

# ~6~

# Love

It's time now to tackle the greatest of these three – love. Let me stress once again, that calling love the greatest, is not to say the others are unimportant. Both faith and hope remain vital, and to have love by itself is not enough. Indeed, as much as it's helpful to separate and understand the distinctive, different qualities of these three motivational characteristics, we must also realise that we rarely, if ever, operate out of just one of these at a time. They interact with, inform and boost each other. In turn, if one area is weak, it can hinder the others, so we must value them as a set. Nevertheless, there is one that stands out that bit brighter, love.

Tackling this subject fills me with a mix of emotions. It feels both easier and harder to write about than any other topic, and I must resign myself now to the knowledge that by the end of the chapter it won't feel like I've done it justice, but who truly can? Knowing this I simply make my goal for this chapter to be a helpful and suitable addition to what we've looked at concerning faith and hope. Now there's always a danger with this sort of book that it could become too 'me-centric', but hopefully you've noticed how God-focused and God-glorifying faith and hope are? Love, of course, is no exception.

Just as with faith and hope, it matters where our love is sourced and focused. Love is not a coverall that makes everything right. For example, the Bible contrasts a love of money vs a love of God. Other examples include being a lover of self, or lover of pleasure.[1] Equally, love cannot justify a wrong relationship and committing adultery. Love that isn't first sourced in God is going to lead you down a wrong path.

By and large, it feels that we don't need to be told how important love is – or maybe we do? Maybe because we can be so familiar with the concept, it becomes easy to brush over, not realising how devoid of love our actions can be? It was undoubtedly an issue for more than one group of people in the Bible who surely should have known better. Certainly, it seems the chief issue for both the Corinthians and the Pharisees was primarily one of the heart, not the head. Concerning the Pharisees, Jesus quoted Isaiah saying:

> *"'These people honour me with their lips,*
>    *but their hearts are far from me.*
> *They worship me in vain;*
>    *their teachings are merely human rules.'"*

Matt 15:8-9 NIV

---

[1]. 2 Tim 3:1-4

The Pharisees were a zealous, God-fearing group, who knew the scriptures far better than most people of the time. But they completely missed the heart and character of the God behind these scriptures. So in turn, for all their knowledge, they often either miss-understood or miss-emphasised what they read and knew. Now don't be deceived, the Pharisees can be treated as a bit of a punch bag at times, and we're shown a lot of their flaws through their interactions with Jesus and His disciples. But we must always look at them as a model and warning of what we the church could so easily become should we miss the heart of God.

But also let's not swing too far the other way. Paul writing to the Philippians said: *"...it is my prayer that your love may abound more and more, with knowledge and all discernment, so that you may approve what is excellent..."*[2] Love needs knowledge and discernment to accompany it, to enable it to be truly helpful and effective. We mustn't let ourselves develop a cosy unreal sense of love being so all-important, that it doesn't matter what you do, as long as it's done in love. Many a painful deed has been done, or hurtful word been spoken with good intentions. The fact that it was motivated by love *might* soften the blow, but it doesn't stop the hit from landing.

Perhaps worse still is making the mistake that the truly awesome love of God summarises His whole character. God is far more complete and complex than that. We trivialise Him if we treat Him as just a doting father who would never

2. Php 1:9

punish wrong beyond a little word or slap on the wrist (if that). Just like us, there are many things, many motivations going on in the heart and head of God. The difference is His are all good and perfectly balanced. Whereas we've got all sorts of rubbish mixed in there, and the good we have may be unhelpfully balanced leading to bad things anyway.

## *Without love*

Whereas the Pharisees thought of themselves as being better than others because of the rules they kept, the Corinthians thought themselves better because of the gifts they had, gifts of the Holy Spirit no less. The root issue for both these groups is that they weren't operating out of love. This fundamental issue robbed their good deeds of their potential value. Even things apparently done in God's name and for His glory were often really done to selfishly boost their own ego's and standing in their different communities. Whether it was making a show and display of the fasting they were doing,[3] or the money they were giving.[4] Or in the Corinthian's case being so desperate to share what God had told them that they wouldn't give space to others who also had something to share.[5] The human ability to take and do good things, then rob them of some of their worth is sadly boundless.

In addressing this issue with the Corinthians, Paul said:

3. Matt 6:16-18
4. Matt 6:1-4
5. 1 Cor 14:29-33

*"... I will show you a still more excellent way.*

*If I speak in the tongues of men and of angels, but have not love, I am a noisy gong or a clanging cymbal. And if I have prophetic powers, and understand all mysteries and all knowledge, and if I have all faith, so as to remove mountains, but have not love, I am nothing. If I give away all I have, and if I deliver up my body to be burned, but have not love, I gain nothing."*

1 Cor 12:31-13:3

I love this, Paul pulls no punches, and we must make sure each one of these three elements has its chance to knock some sense into us where needed.

## Noise

*"If I speak in the tongues of men and of angels, but have not love, I am a noisy gong or a clanging cymbal."*

The human voice is a wonderful gift. With it we sing great and wonderful songs, we communicate important truths, and we can try and build each other up. But if you do any of this is without love, you're just a noise. A loud banging noise. It doesn't matter how good your singing voice is, or how good a communicator you are, without love you're just a racket in someone's ear. That's God assessment of you. But not only His, this is something we can feel towards others as well. When a person is speaking to you, whether a teacher on a platform, or someone giving you some advice face to face, if you sense it's coming out of a bad heart it's very easy to just shut down, stop listening, and they become little more than an annoying clatter going around inside your head. If we want to do others good with our voice, the first and most important act we must attend to is assessing our heart. If the motive of love isn't there, we'd do well to hold back until it is. As is often said in different ways: "unless they know that you care, they won't care what you say".

It should be noted, however, that this will be a matter of perception, and perceptions can be wrong. You might receive an encouragement or criticism given genuinely in love, worded thoughtfully and well. But instead of hearing it as intended, you immediately become offended and the barriers go up. Or maybe you yourself have said something which was taken completely in the wrong way. Whichever side of this you find yourself on you need to remember this key principle: *You're responsible for your heart, not theirs.*

The first step in being responsible for your own heart is testing your motives. Ask yourself why you want to challenge this person. As a rule, the majority us don't relish bringing a challenge to others, but we all need good friends who are willing, indeed loving enough to do this. And if we need others to do this for us, we certainly need to be ready and able to do it for them. As Solomon says in Proverbs: *"Faithful are the wounds of a friend..."*[6] Love is both the

6. Prov 27:6

best motive and the great balancer in these situations. For those perhaps a little too willing or simply hasty in challenging others, love helps to put the brakes on and make sure due care is taken, for love is not rude. And for those more timid, love builds up the courage required to step out and do something uncomfortable but needed for their friends' sake. It is sometimes misunderstood that love would most likely just lets things pass unchallenged, and there are indeed occasions when in loving patience you should indeed just let something go. But in truth, for those of us at the timid end of things, it's frequently fear that holds us back rather than love letting something pass. Love is willing to wound if it will ultimately help. This is just another way in which *love proves to be truly kind.*

It's worth noting before moving on one other aspect of testing your own heart. Are you guilty of the same kind of mistakes? Jesus warned of judging others concerning things you also struggle with *"Why do you see the speck that is in your brother's eye, but do not notice the log that is in your own eye..."*[7] (Parents – take particular note with this concerning how your talk to your children). Before you challenge someone else, take time to assess if this is something you struggle with in some way. Indeed, ask God to reveal it to you in case you're too blind to see it. He's certainly shown me a few things through such prayers. Once done, you're in a better place for talking to your friend. And even if you do have a similar issue to address, that doesn't necessarily mean you can't bring the challenge. But it will

---

7. Matt 6:3

(or should) affect the way you bring it, adding that bit more humility and honesty to your conversation, for *love is not proud*.

With all this done, if your words are not well received, it is worth taking the time to reflect if you should have handled it differently. Again, love is not proud. If appropriate consult another trustworthy and neutral person. But if it proves all due care has been taken, take heart, and try not to let it put you off, for you were being a loving, faithful friend. Continue to pray for them, and remember, you're responsible for your heart, not theirs.

On the other side of this is receiving. How do you respond to challenges from others? Just as few people relish the thought of confronting others, there are probably even less who like to be confronted. It can at the very least be uncomfortable if not painful, even when said in the wisest most loving of ways. Once again, our job is to be responsible for our own heart's reaction. And love's response must be to presume the best of them, even if the challenge may have come without any *perceived* tact, love, or even understanding. Remember, *love is not irritable or easily angered*. In these circumstances, it's a good habit to go gold-digging. Search through what was said and see what nuggets of truth there may be that you can latch on to and work with to challenge yourself. On the other hand, if it has been done well, responding well is usually much easier. Love is not proud, and so it can take a wound, a faithful rebuke from caring friend, and do something good with it.

Furthermore, when you find yourself on the receiving end, consider even thanking your friend for having the courage to do this. *For love does not delight in evil, but rejoices with the truth.* I genuinely thank God for friends that will take the trouble to faithfully wound me, and I ask for the courage to be so faithful myself.

### Being Somebody

*"And if I have prophetic powers, and understand all mysteries and all knowledge, and if I have all faith, so as to remove mountains, but have not love, I am nothing."*

It is, no doubt, not a new phenomenon at all, but it can feel like there's an even greater push these days for people to try and find both their identity and worth in all the wrong places, through all the wrong means. It might be through sporting or business success, getting married and having children, living in the best area, having all the latest stuff, or being really important within a certain community? The church doesn't live free of this either, with any of the above creeping in to claim a value or be a driving force that they shouldn't be. Even positions of responsibility and influence within a church can be sought for all the wrong reasons. And if Paul was hard-hitting in his last charge of calling people just a noise, he's absolutely scathing now as he basically calls them a nobody! It doesn't matter how successful you've been, how wise you are, how much you know or how skilled and gifted you may be – without love, you're nothing, no one.

I hope you didn't move onto this next paragraph too quickly? Make sure you take that in because it's so easy to shake it off and not let it have its due impact. There are too many people both outside and inside the church who are seeking to be 'someone', but the way they're going about it makes them a 'no-one' in God's assessment.

Now we have another important principle to absorb: there is no direct or automatic link between gifting and character – none! Even when that gifting is a spiritual gift. It's good, essential even, to recognise God's anointing on people and to enable them to put it to good use for His glory and praise. But it's equally vital that we first also recognise good character in them before they're given authority and ministries in which to use these gifts. If the gift is there, but not the character they're not ready yet, and you must wait for both to be there before appointing people. Sadly there are some who don't see the need to grow in character first and so never get the full opportunity to step out into all that God has for them. Possibly worse still are those who *are* given the opportunity before they're ready. It's only a matter of time before this bad character will be exposed, risking God's name being tarnished in the minds of others and good works being needlessly undone. You can't of course wait for them to be perfect. That remains solely God's domain, and we're all still a work in progress. But that too I'd argue is part of the character we should be looking for – someone who's looking to grow and isn't content to stay just as they are.

Before we move on, I'd just like to acknowledge how Paul does slightly soften these blows to the Corinthian's. He doesn't actually say: "you're just a noise speaking like that", but rather: "If *I speak*... but have not love, *I am* a noisy gong..." And he doesn't say: "despite all you're your gifts, you're a nobody", but rather "...if *I have* prophetic powers, and understand all mysteries... but have not love, *I am* nothing." Paul made it initially personal to him rather than directly condemning any of them, whilst still making the point quite clear. Perhaps he's aware of how easy it would be, having the heritage that he has, and the immense Spiritual giftings, to fall for the lie that it's this that gives him his worth and makes him 'somebody'? *For love, of course, does not boast*, it does not focus on these things. Luke's gospel records when Jesus sent out in pairs seventy-two of His disciples to proclaim the Kingdom of God and heal the sick. They returned to Him jubilant saying *"Lord, even the demons are subject to us in your name!"*[8] Jesus affirms them and what had happened but also seeks to make sure they're centred correctly. He says to them: *"Nevertheless, do not rejoice in this, that the spirits are subject to you, but rejoice that your names are written in heaven"*.[9] Please don't think that Jesus is being a killjoy here. He does want them to rejoice, and acknowledge the incredible stuff that they're seeing and doing, but He wants

8. Luke 10:17
9. Luke 10:20

their rejoicing centred on their standing before God, before how He's including them in His great work. In this way, He's helping to steer them away from the potential perils of becoming full of themselves, rather than full of God.

Now Paul's challenge to the Corinthian's, and in turn to us, is not to bring us down low, but to encourage us to humbly rise up in a better way. You want to be 'someone'? Brilliant! Then learn to love with zeal and humility. Train your heart in Godly loving ways, and allow it to influence and motivate you're every move. Then you will truly be a 'somebody'.

## Gain

*"If I give away all I have, and if I deliver up my body to be burned, but have not love, I gain nothing."*

Of Paul's three quick 'punches' at the Corinthian's values, this one is surely the most surprising - I *gain* nothing. Following the logic of the previous two punches: without love, I'm just a loud annoying noise – but with love, I'm worth listening to; without love, I'm nothing – with love I am someone; and so now, without love, I gain nothing – but with love, I gain something. Is it right to mix the motive of love with the motive of seeking gain? Indeed, does love itself seek gain? Isn't that really selfishness instead of love? If we're treating Paul's letter to the Corinthian's as God's word (which I hope you do), then surely we must conclude that love truly does seek gain, along with seeking to speak in ways that bless and aren't just noise; and seeking to be a person of worth – truly a 'somebody' in the very best sense.

To move forwards we must address the question: how can genuine love seek gain whilst not being selfish? Consider fear for a moment. We're told many times in the Bible to fear God and the benefits of doing so.[10] But we're also told in John's first letter that "perfect love casts out fear."[11] So how do we reconcile these two things? Well, I can't claim to understand it all yet, but it would seem that there is a right and healthy way to fear God and a wrong and unhealthy way. I believe the best way to test which fear you have (if any), is to examine the effect it has on you. The unhealthy fear will leave you afraid and not wanting to be near God. A healthy fear of God will be faith born, and leave you wanting to draw closer to Him.

Similarly, there is a right and healthy way to seek gain and a wrong and unhealthy way. Let's take a very basic everyday example – food. We all want to be able to eat and drink each day. Our body needs this, and to seek this 'gain' is no bad thing. We don't condemn people for this, and indeed many of us take it for granted. There is nothing in and of itself wrong about seeking gain. Selfishness, however, *seeks gain at the expense*, or at best in ignorance of others. It either doesn't care, or doesn't stop to think about the effect it has on other people. Concerning their practice of the Lord's Supper, Paul had to chastise the

---

10. For example: Luke 1:50; Rom 3:18; 11:20; 2 Cor 5:11 and more besides
11. 1 John 4:18; (Rom 8:15 also points to this)

Corinthian's, even going as far as saying that it could no longer be considered a Lord's Supper because *"...in eating, each one goes ahead with his own meal. One goes hungry, another gets drunk. What! Do you not have houses to eat and drink in? Or do you despise the church of God and humiliate those who have nothing?"*[12] Once again, a sad example of humankind taking a good, God-given thing and utterly ruining it. And the root cause? Selfishness.

In contrast to this, we have love. And the contrast is not that love doesn't seek gain, but that it seeks gain *in the benefit of others*. Allow me a moment of fatherly pride here. Recently we had a little report from school concerning one of my daughters' behaviour. In it, the teacher wrote "[She] has been very busy this morning making cakes (play dough ones) for both her friends and teachers. *She always finds joy in making other people feel happy*." There in a nutshell, you have a great example of the nature of love. It seeks joy in making other people feel happy. Now some will argue that love may *find* joy (as if by accident) in blessing others, but would never actually *seek* its own joy. But I don't think that adds up with all that I find in the Bible or indeed what I experience in life. There's another name for doing things that bless others without feeling and simply for the sake of doing that thing – duty. Duty is a good and helpful thing, but we've been shown a better way – love. Love feels and seeks gain, not at the expense of others, and not as a neutral party, but in the benefit of others.

---

12.   1 Cor 11:22

This is a really important aspect of love to grasp, so let me dwell on this for a while. If the thought of seeking your own gain turns you off as horrible thing to do, I encourage you to try reading through the Bible again whilst looking for this sort of thing, for you will find it, and not just here and there. Seeking gain in some form is a surprisingly common motivator used in the Bible. God doesn't seem to simply want our motivation to be good for goods own sake, but first for God's sake and then for our own. Because we love Him, and because we see that His way truly is the best, and the way that will bring the most gain, most joy.

Consider the most loving act of all time, Jesus Christ willingly, and purposefully died on a cross for you and me. He suffered humiliation, immense physical pain, and in ways that (praise God) those of us who believe in Him will never experience – the wrath of God over sin. Why? Because of love! And as the writer of Hebrews puts it: *"...for the joy that was set before him endured the cross, despising the shame..."*[13] Joy, not duty was His motivation. And what joy was this? A joy in obedience to the Father and His will, whom He loves to please. A joy in saving many souls in such a surprising and perfect way, that served justice, honoured God and made sinners righteous. For those who would go on to believe in Him, it released them to a whole new and immeasurably better life. Should that not fill Him with joy? Should He not seek His own joy through such a *selfless* act!?

---

13. Heb 12:2

Now let me take you to Romans:

> *"God 'will repay each person according to what they have done.' To those who by persistence in doing good seek glory, honour and immortality, he will give eternal life. But those who are self-seeking and who reject the truth and follow evil, there will be wrath and anger."*

> Romans 2:6-8 NIV

The good and loving actions of this first group are done seeking after glory, honour and immortality. Does God rebuke them for a self-seeking attitude? No! He gives them exactly what they're seeking – eternal life. They're the ones genuinely living out of love. It's the next group that are accused of being self-seeking, who in turn reject the truth and follow evil.

Consider also Paul's encouragement to the Corinthian's about giving:

> *"The point is this: whoever sows sparingly will also reap sparingly, and whoever sows bountifully will also reap bountifully. Each one must give as he has decided in his heart, not reluctantly or under compulsion, for God loves a cheerful giver."*

> 2 Cor 9:6-7

First of all, we have a distinct appeal to the heart to do a good thing in order to gain. In this case, he's talking about giving money to others in need, though the principle can surely be applied more broadly: Sow sparingly, and you'll reap little. Sow bountifully, and you'll reap much. The picture of sowing is helpful in that it indicates an investment and patient waiting to reap the fruit (and it may be that only some or none is reaped in this life). But notice that the enticement, the motive encouraged, is to seek more gain. Furthermore giving, or doing the good deed out of a sense of obligation is positively discouraged. God's looking for cheerful givers, not dutiful ones. Those who see the need and give out of the overflow of their heart, even if their own resources aren't overflowing.

Let's look at a different area where this is less obvious. We looked at the 'faithful wounds of a friend' earlier in the chapter, and we find a similar situation in parenting. Disciplining my children is no fun, not for them or me. It gives me no pleasure to do it, and them no pleasure to receive it. Yet I would not be loving my children well if I failed to do this for them. Sometimes (often) they need to be told 'no', or to face consequences for their bad behaviour. So where's the love sought gain in that? It's in the character of my ever-growing children. The love sought joy set before us as parents in these situations is one of delayed gratification. It's in the slow but ever-developing maturity of those we're responsible for, as we watch and play a key part in them growing into wonderful young men and women, so full of potential and, all being well, of good character. For in this, we know that they too will be far happier individuals if their character blossoms into something genuinely beautiful. This is something that will give us so much joy and gratitude as they reach maturity. And the cost? The cost is in our lovingly making the painful effort to train and discipline them as best we can, whilst we have both the opportunity and responsibility. So here too we find love seeking gain, in and for the benefit of others. This might also be an example of love "*always hoping*" from Paul's great description of love in 1 Corinthians, as it looks to the future good in/of others?

Finally, let me put it this way. In the end, love is about assigning true value. When we love others, we're putting a worth on them in our minds, so in turn, their benefit and happiness becomes our gain too, because they've become a treasure to us.

## *The Source*

Please note that I've purposefully not tried to define love in this chapter. I've never found anything or been able to come up with a definition that completely satisfies me. Not even the apostle Paul seems to attempt this, instead, we get that beautiful (but not exhaustive) description of love (which we will finally get to at the end of this chapter). However, I am very fond of the way John Piper summed it up in his book Desiring God. "*Love is the overflow of joy in God that gladly meets the needs of others*".[14] Now if you

14. John Piper, Desiring God, p119, 2003

were unconvinced about what I said in the last section, or simply want to consider it more, let me direct you to the book where this quote comes from and particularly his chapter on love. Once I'd processed, understood and become convinced of what he teaches in that chapter, the whole rest of the book became much easier to read and grasp. But back to the subject in hand – what I love about that quote is how rich it is in meaning, with some very choice words quickly summing up a lot of thought. The second half 'gladly meeting the needs of others', was essentially looked at in the last section. Now we take a step back to look at 'the overflow'. You cannot give what you do not have. And you cannot overflow unless you're continuously getting filled. Thankfully, as the apostle John explains, we have the greatest source of love:

> *"In this is love, not that we have loved God but that he loved us and sent his Son to be the propitiation for our sins. Beloved, if God so loved us, we also ought to love one another."*

1 John 4:10-11

This is where we must always start if we want to grow in love, not in trying harder to love God or others, but in turning to both the foundation and fountain of it all – that God first loved us. He made the first move, He initiated the relationship we can now have with Him, He made that first loving step. And what an incredible step it was. He sent His Son to be the propitiation for our sins. That is to say, to be the appeasement, the offering that satisfies God on every level, and enables Him to justly release us from our debt of sin.

If you struggle to respond in love to God and others, this is where you must start. Pray and ask God to help you see and feel the immense and intense love He has for you. To help you understand just how far He came for you and the raging, heartfelt zeal behind it. Oh, God's love is tender too, patient, kind and all these wonderful things. But it is not merely nice, and it's certainly not soppy. *"For God so loved the world, that He gave His only son"*.[15] He *so* loved us that He gave that which is most precious to Him. God's love is indescribably passionate, entirely sober, and joyfully lavish. And because we have this incomprehensible Holy Trinity which is our God, we can also say that God died in our place, Jesus Christ the Son of God died for me! *"Greater love has no one than this, that someone lay down his life for his friends."*[16]

If we don't feel the depths of this, are we too familiar with the words? What's the saying? 'Familiarity breeds contempt'. I must confess that sometimes I wonder if my heart has simply become dull, dry and slow with familiarity? These great truths that my heart once leapt for joy over, are they now nothing more than head knowledge? Sadly there is probably some truth in this at times, and a bit of taking God's love for granted in an unhelpful sense. But there's something else going on too. Remember as we've already explored, love is not a feeling, it's a motive or a

15. John 3:16
16. John 15:13

motivational characteristic. And so analysing whether God's love is impacting us or not is going to involve a 'what and why' type question. What do I do and why? How am I living my life in light of His love? I've been married for a good number of years now (seven when first writing this). I'll openly admit that my feelings for my wife are not felt in quite the same way as when we first started going out. My love for her is no less strong, actually I'd say its stronger. But the giddy side has diminished, and been replaced with something else, something hard to do justice in describing, but here goes – it's a more homely, comfortable feeling. There's no one I want to spend more time with, no one I feel more accepted by, no one I want to please more, and no one I feel more at home with wherever we might be. And you'll find evidence of this in my actions and decisions – making sure I get to spend regular quality time with her, and doing things I know make her happy, be it getting jobs done I'm supposed to or doing things together.

Similarly with God, though He does bless me with times where it all seems so fresh and new, and I'm blown over by the love felt. But much of the time I'm operating out of a similar place to where I'm at with my wife. It's not a giddy feeling, but it is a sober passion. It remains (sadly and inevitably) meagre and woefully lacking compared to His love for me, but it is certainly there. How can we properly test this? We can't rely merely on feelings for such a test (though they remain important in different ways). I'd suggest asking yourself how you do in these three areas:

*Firstly, Making time for Him.* Where does God stand in your priorities from day to day? Is He someone you want to spend time with? Do you make an effort to make sure this happens? Do you miss Him, and regret it if you don't on any given day?

*Secondly, Obedience.* Jesus said: *"If you love me, you will keep my commandments."*[17] It's easy to forget that this is an expected result of love, we can link it more to fearing God than loving Him. Indeed, this one by itself may not be from love at all, it could be all motivated by fear or mere legalism. None of these three things by themselves are a good indicator of your love for God. All three need to be looked at together as a whole. And part of that whole that you're looking for is the desire to please Him through doing what He says.

*Thirdly and finally, Loving others*, and in particular His people. This one, in part, flows out of the second. As Jesus said to His followers: *"This is my commandment, that you love one another as I have loved you."*[18] And then in John's first letter we read: *"If anyone says, "I love God," and hates his brother, he is a liar; for he who does not love his brother whom he has seen cannot love God whom he has not seen. And this commandment we have from him: whoever loves God must also love his brother."*[19] It is simply a natural progression or consequence that if we truly love God we will love those that He loves, we will love our brothers and sisters in Christ, who have been bought with the same blood, shed on the same cross, with whom we are now made family

17. John 14:15
18. John 15:12
19. 1 John 4:20-21

(hence being 'brothers and sisters'). So how do you treat your fellow Christians? The respect, concern, and care you show for them, in both word and deed, will be a significant indicator of your love for God Himself.

> *"... if we love one another, God abides in us and his love is perfected in us."*
>
> *1 John 4:12*

### The Greatest

As a rule, most of the Pharisees and Scribes of Jesus time did not like Him. Some of it was jealousy as to His popularity among the people, some of it was in His actions, and much of it was because of His teaching, exposing wrong thoughts and attitudes. But there were some exceptions including one Scribe, who after witnessing several people try and trap Jesus with clever questions, instead decided to ask Him a more meaningful one.

> *"...one of the scribes came up and heard them disputing with one another, and seeing that he answered them well, asked him, "Which commandment is the most important of all?" Jesus answered, "The most important is, 'Hear, O Israel: The Lord our God, the Lord is one. And you shall love the Lord your God with all your heart and with all your soul and with all your mind and with all your strength.' The second is this: 'You shall love your neighbour as yourself.' There is no other commandment greater than these." And the scribe*

> *said to him, "You are right, Teacher. You have truly said that he is one, and there is no other besides him. And to love him with all the heart and with all the understanding and with all the strength, and to love one's neighbour as oneself, is much more than all whole burnt offerings and sacrifices." And when Jesus saw that he answered wisely, he said to him, "You are not far from the kingdom of God." And after that no one dared to ask him any more questions."*

*Mark 12:28-34*

You get the impression that this Scribe's question was still a sort of test for Jesus, but one coming from a more genuine heart, more ready to accept Him if the answer was good, rather than simply trying to trap Jesus. The answer of course, was spot on, and the Scribe knew it. It's a nice place to leave this little episode. After a variety of people coming at Jesus with a bad heart and hidden motives, we end with one who may just come around to believe in Him? It should be noted also, that Jesus was not teaching a completely new thing or concept (at least it shouldn't have been new to people's ears), as He was quoting from the scriptures they already had, in particular, Deuteronomy (6:4-6) and Leviticus (19:18). Jesus didn't come and change this, He brought to light what was already there, but that had been missed by many. The two key commandments that summarise them all, and more than that, they put the right heart behind them. So, we see that love is both the greatest of the core motivators and is behind the greatest of God's commandments. We're to love God with all our heart, soul, mind and strength. With our all. I love God, I really do, but there is no commandment that so starkly highlights to me how far short I fall. Praise God for Christ Jesus paying my debt of sin on that cross! But where do we go from here? With our debt paid, we still want to change and lead lives worthy of the calling upon them – to love God and others more and more. How do we change and grow? We've already looked at the source of our love, and resting in God's love for us must always be the first step if we're to start right with the best foundations. Thankfully our help doesn't stop there either, as the Holy Spirit now works in us to change us from within, and love is the first of the fruit, the first evidence of His growing in us listed in Galatians.[20] But still, what can we do?

> *"For those who live according to the flesh set their minds on the things of the flesh, but those who live according to the Spirit set their minds on the things of the Spirit."*

*Romans 8:5*

Now don't think of your mind as being your purely logical side. Trust me, you and your mind are not fully logical. But we do have a control over our minds that we don't have with our desires or emotions. We all have a mixture of desires going on inside us, some good, some bad, and all sorts of emotions going on alongside this. The

20. Gal 5:22

question is what are you going to do with them? What's required of us is to set our minds (the element we do control) on the things of the Spirit – on what He desires, on what is good and right and Godly. And in so doing this we start to train our desires, feeding the good and hopefully starving the bad. Here we find an ongoing principle in the Bible. If you want to change, don't just try to cut out the bad, but also replace it with something good. So here it's both taking our minds off wrong and ungodly desires, and putting them on what the Spirit desires, on what is good. So for example, if you struggle with gossip and have a habit of slandering people behind their back, don't just try and stop doing that, but make a conscious decision and effort to speak well of people and build them up. Not just when they're not around, but encourage them to their face. In this way, you'll start to change from being someone who tears down in secret, to someone who builds up in public. You've moved from setting your mind on things that the 'flesh' so often craves, to things that the Holy Spirit within you desires. You've got behind and worked alongside the Spirit, and so, in turn, have become a more loving person.

### *How to grow old*

Let me share with you in good length, one of my favourite stories of someone who embodied a life of love and was still growing in this as she got ever older. Evelyn was born in England in 1879, the ninth of eleven children. From early on it was evident that she had a very independent character, with a love of colours, painting and all living things. At the age of thirty, Evelyn announced to her family that God had called her to become a missionary to India. Her dad, not wanting her to go, insisted that she get checked out by a doctor first, to make sure she'd be physically capable of living in the tropics without harm to her health. She passed with flying colours. Evelyn was not the flimsy petal her beautiful and fashionable dresses could make her seem. She was made of tougher stuff, and her dad relented, having to concede that she must follow God's will above his own.

Assigned to the Madras region of India, she went about her training, learning languages and some medical skills among other things. Here she met the same young man, Jesse Brand, whose talk God had used to call her to the mission field. They soon found they were of a kindred spirit, and together embarked on a mission to bring the gospel to a region of five mountain ranges that had become known as the 'Mountains of Death'.[21] They were married in sight of the Kolli mountain range, and the very next day set off together for their new home, which Jesse had built up on the hill ready for them. They spent their time teaching better farming methods, treating the sick, helping build houses for the poorest, and of course teaching the people there about God. Except for one death bed conversion early on, they went seven years without seeing anyone saved. Seven years

---

21. A collection of five mountain ranges; the Kollis (where they started), Pachais, Kalrayan, Peria Malai, and Chitteris

of what might feel like failure, but they persisted in love and faith. The turning point came when a Hindu priest who carried great influence and who had been adamantly against them caught the fever. Jesse and Evelyn hurried to his aid. As he died, the priest entrusted his children to the Brands. 'The Jesus God must be the true one', he said, because the Brands alone had helped him in his hour of death.

Jesse and Evelyn continued together for another thirteen years of slow but productive ministry, helping many people, and started to see more and more people saved, before Jesse himself succumbed to Blackwater Fever. Evelyn was devastated and everyone, it seemed, expected her to go back home at this point. But that was not on her mind. She felt God wanted her to complete the task she and her husband had started. Now at fifty years old, she spends the next twenty continuing to work for the mission in India on the Kolli hills. At sixty-nine, she sought to start a new work in the Kalryans, but was denied by the missions board, because she was old, single, and possibly because she was so stubbornly opinionated. She'd given the mission board trouble on several occasions, and they weren't for budging on this. Evelyn clutched at one last straw. 'Please just send me back for one last year,' she pleaded. 'I promise not to make any more trouble.' The board relented, and in this final year with the help of her two children, she smuggled in materials and had a little bungalow built for herself in the mountains. Her final year with the mission ended; fellow missionaries gathered to wish her a tearful good-bye. But Evelyn told them gleefully that she wasn't going home.

Instead, she bought a pony and started travelling from village to village in the Kalryans, sharing the gospel and loving people in whatever way she could. Finally, she'd been able to start bringing the gospel to the second of five mountain ranges that she and Jesse had always dreamed of reaching.

She spent another twenty-three years travelling from village to village loving people, becoming known as Granny Brand. Broken bones, sickness, ageing, her battles with the marijuana growers... it seemed nothing would stop her. With the help of a growing group of people, she brought the message of the gospel to the five mountain ranges, and a further two beyond.[22] At the age of ninety she was on a trip back to the Kollis, and the place where it all started for her. This time she had her niece, Dr Ruth, for company. To Evelyn's surprise, her memories of the place were no longer marred with bitterness towards the mission board, which from her point of view, had both neglected and compromised the work which she and Jesse had started. The matter had simply become unimportant to her anymore. Her son Paul had noticed this change in her just a few months prior. In a letter, he wrote that he'd found her "distinctly younger than she was a year ago." At first, this puzzled him as she was not physically any stronger. But then 'he put his finger on it' – for many years her love for these hill people had been contending within her with an anger towards those

---

22. The Bothais and Paithur hills

she felt had hindered the work. Now it seemed her love had been able to extend further still to include those who had unintentionally, perhaps not been so helpful in the work being done there? The result was a peace and inner strength that made her shine all the more. "This is how to grow old," Paul had written, "Allow everything else to fall away, until those around you see just love. They will also see your own life renewed and they will recognise the love, to be the love of God."

At ninety-three years old she was still going, still pushing with what strength remained in her frail body to care for others and share the wonderful story of Jesus Christ. Becoming too unbalanced to ride a donkey anymore, men from the surrounding villages came and put her in a hammock and carried her from village to village because they loved her so much. Through this, she was enabled to keep teaching and telling the story of her beloved Jesus for another two years. Two years more lived and given as a gift of love, carried in a hammock, doing whatever she still could to help the poorest of the poor. She continued this work nearly to her very dying day, when the Lord finally brought His good and faithful servant home.[23]

## *Record keeping*

I love this story of Evelyn 'Granny' Brand. I quoted her son near the beginning of this book: "This is how to grow

---

23. For a fuller account of Evelyn's story, I can recommend: Dorothy Clarke Wilson, Granny Brand Her Story, 1976

old…" And finally reading a fuller account of her story put this quote of his into its proper context for me. This wonderfully loving lady just kept growing in character, and now it seemed she had learned to forgive those she had viewed as obstructing, or at the very least being unhelpful to the work she and her late husband had started. The result was a new youthfulness added to this ninety-year-old. If I live to be that old, I dearly want to be someone who is still growing in character and wisdom with God. What needless weight we carry when we fail to forgive. It seems that it does more harm to us than to those we hold the grudge against.

*Love keeps no record of wrongs* we're told. Yet in this, I do wonder if we sometimes teach this slightly wrong and take it a little too far. What I mean is, we read something like: "*For I will be merciful toward their iniquities, and I will remember their sins no more.*"[24] And take it to mean that God literally forgets our sin. Like He gives Himself amnesia just in this precise area. Then you get teaching that encourages you by saying: "You don't need to say to God sorry for sinning in this way yet *again*, because He literally can't remember the last time after He forgave you." Forgive and forget? But is that truly the dynamic going on between us and God? My impression (and of course I could be wrong – impressions/feelings do not trump the authority of scripture), is that as I interact with God and bring to Him my confessions, He isn't oblivious to the fact that I have ongoing issues, or that He's had to forgive me about this

---

24. Heb 8:12

before. He hasn't forgotten, but He has forgiven and does not *count* them against me.

Let me try and illustrate this in another way. I was horrified with myself one morning when I realised that when I saw one of my daughters for the first time that day, I was not looking at them with the eyes of fatherly love but with condemnation. Her behaviour the previous evening had, let's just say, not been good. I had not yet forgiven her, and my mercies were not new that morning like God's were. I had kept a record in my head and heart. Quickly and internally I turned to God, asking Him to forgive my unforgiveness, my petty grudge against my own beautiful daughter! Furthermore, I asked the Spirit to help me properly forgive her, in which He was quick and eager to oblige.

Now my role as a father means that I have a key part to play in helping my children grow up into people of good character. To do this well, I need to be aware of where they struggle, to be able to see the difference between patterns of behaviour and blips along the way. If I literally forget what they've done I can't do this, and so I cannot help them so well. What I need is not to forget, but to not keep a record. There's a subtle yet substantial difference here. In not keeping record I'm not keeping it against them, I'm not there ready to bring back their whole past upon them, and perhaps most importantly, when I look at them, I'm not seeing their flaws, but the wonderfully and fearfully God-made person that He has graciously put in my life. A person

He's put there for me to love, cherish, and ultimately release into the world with all the potential they have within. It's all about how we view people. Do we just see the flaws and let that define our image of them? Or do we see the person with eyes of love, valuing them? Not holding a record of past sins against them, but neither being blind and silly, pretending that they're perfect as they are.

When my loving Heavenly Father looks at me, I know that He does not see all my sins heaped up against me, for He has truly removed them as far as the east is from the west.[25] But neither is He under any illusions as to my current condition. I'm growing and getting better by His Holy Spirit at work in me, and one day, when He brings this life to a close and gives me a new body, I will finally be made perfect and totally free from sin in every sense. Maybe its at that point when the work is complete, He will truly remember my sins no more? Until that day He knowingly, and patiently continues His good work of transformation in me. Praise God.

### *A good ambition*

I've purposefully not delved into Paul's beautiful description of love found in 1 Corinthians. It just never seemed like the right thing to do for this chapter, but I hope you noted the semi-frequent references to it. Now as this chapter draws to a close, I encourage you to read Paul's

---

25. Psalm 103:12

words anew, delight in them, cherish them. Then make it your ambition, through the work of the Holy Spirit, to make these words a more and more accurate description of you with each year of life that passes. Indeed, letting all else fall away till all that remains is love. For…

> *"Love is patient, love is kind. It does not envy, it does not boast, it is not proud. It does not dishonour others, it is not self-seeking, it is not easily angered, it keeps no record of wrongs. Love does not delight in evil, but rejoices with the truth. It always protects, always trusts, always hopes, and always perseveres."*
>
> 1 Corinthians 13:4-7 NIV

# ~7~

# The Who and The Why

*"In the beginning was the Word, and the Word was with God, and the Word was God."*

John 1:1

It's quite an opening that John gave to his gospel. He dives straight into defining something of the divine and eternal nature of Jesus Christ, the Word. It's an intriguing beginning, with a possible extra aspect to John's thinking that isn't immediately evident. John spent much of his life-based in Ephesus, and it's believed he was there when he wrote this gospel. There had been a well-known Greek philosopher also based in Ephesus, who was active around 500 BC. His name was Heraclitus; he believed in the importance of scientific enquiry, and the search to discover how and why the natural world behaves as it does. In his studies, he used the word 'logos' to stand for 'the reason why'. So, for whatever he was investigating, he would say that he was looking for the 'logos.' This is the same Greek word that we translate as the 'Word' in John's gospel. Was this in John's mind as he wrote? We can't know for sure, but it is certainly true that Jesus Christ is the ultimate reason behind all creation. He was there in the beginning, He was with God, and He was God. He is God, and it was He who spoke our world and the whole universe into existence in all its vast spans and minute detail. It is He that gave life its meaning, its mechanisms and its rules. Jesus Christ is the 'why' of all creation.

In turn, God desires to become your 'why', the very reason you do what you do, the reason that you live the way you live. And yet more than that, God wants to be the person that defines you! It's so easy to get caught up in the many ways the world wants to define itself. And there are so many! Through jobs, the music you like, sports teams you support, or political parties. Through where you live, your sexuality, the clothes you wear, the food you eat or don't eat. It's not like this is all completely unimportant, but it's a pretty superficial way of defining yourself. How much more sensible and freeing to let our creator God be the one who defines us from the centre of our being. The One who knew us before we were even born.[1] The only One who truly understands how we're made and what our potential is. The only One capable of judging us fairly, in complete knowledge and righteousness[2], and without hypocrisy. The only One able to pay our debt of sin, before all accounts are called in to be settled.[3] Isn't it better to have the creator of all things define us rather than something/anything that He has created?

1. Jer 1:5
2. Rom 2:16, Rev 19:11
3. Col 2:14

God wants you to be defined by a faith, hope and love rooted and sustained in Him. This, in turn, will overflow to motivate your every word and deed, bringing glory to God, satisfaction to your soul, and blessing those around you. But if you choose, you can put your faith, hope and love in other things, and if you do, it's those things that will start to define you. This is why it's so important to source them in God alone. You can choose to put your faith and hope in wealth. If so, your security will be based on your bank balance, a very insecure foundation, which even if abundant in this life, will be worth nothing in the next. No, worse than that, it will be a millstone around your neck, pronouncing your own judgement – that you considered money as something greater than God Himself. Love also is not automatically a good all covering thing. Just because you love someone, it won't make up for or cover over anything if it's a wrong relationship. To think this way is to make feelings god, and it becomes simply another form of idolatry along with the love of money. There are endless examples of what we can put in God's rightful place, but none of them will fulfil our soul or bring honour to God. So many good things, used in bad ways for evil reasons.

This book has aimed to help us to see the key role that God wants faith, hope, and love play in our lives. To understand something of how they affect and motivate us from our core outwards. And to encourage a desire to see more of them all at work within us. These three things, that have as much worth in the next life as they do in this one.

These three things that we really can take with us. If I've been able to encourage you to press forwards in this, let me leave you with three things to remember.

### *Remember where you're going*

Or put another way, remember you're in a process. You're not defined by what you do, what you've done, or by what you're like now. But rather by where you're heading, and what you've been declared to be. You may have been reading this whilst feeling very aware of the faults in your own life. Maybe things that you've struggled with for some time? You've tried and failed for so long that you start to wonder if God has given up on you? But who are you to presume God has given up on you? Do you know His mind? Get up! Repent, take heart, and get moving. Consider the order in which God is dealing with your sin.

1) He pays our debt of sin and declares us righteous – justified.
   We not only have our debt paid but Christ's own righteousness credited to our account received through faith in Christ Jesus and His sacrifice for us. We're born again in spirit, ready to start a new life.
2) He gives us hope – the promise of a future life completely without sin. New bodies, and ultimately a new earth. A complete and utter change that will see

## THE WHO AND THE WHY 135

us transformed so as never to see or experience sin again. Finally, eternally, and fully free. This is of course the final stage. We have to wait for the fulfilment of this, but the promise, the expectation of this comes first.

3) Then He begins in earnest, the process of sanctification. We're slowly but surely being transformed, day by day, year by year, *"from one degree of glory to another"*.[4] This is a lifelong process. You should not expect to have it all worked out yet. You will not move into the fulfilment of the promise – complete freedom from sin in every sense – until either death, or Christ returns and we're changed in an instant.[5]

Let's put this another way. We are saved in all three tenses. We have been saved (from the penalty of sin), we will be saved (from the presence of sin), and we are being saved (from the influence of sin). And it's perhaps helpful to remember it in that order.

We're not of course left to our own devices as we continue to battle with 'the flesh' as the Bible often puts it, with the influence that sin still has in our lives. We're saved by faith, given a hope, and given a Helper – The Holy Spirit. And what a beautiful mystery that is. We get filled with the Holy Spirit and become His temple. When the Spirit of God fell upon the temple that the Israelites had built, it was a joyous and terrifying thing. God is awesome and not to be

---

4. 2 Cor 3:18
5. 1 Cor 15:51-52

trifled with or taken lightly. It's this same God that now dwells in us who believe and have received Him, the same God for whom all things are possible[6]. Therefore, your next step – your next battle to grow and become more like the person He made you to be is always possible. And one day He'll take you through that final and wonderful step, in an instant. And sin will be only in your history, never again in your presence.

Ruth Graham (the wife of the famous evangelist Billy Graham) died in 2007. The words she requested to be engraved on her gravestone had nothing to do with any of her many achievements. It had to do with the fact that as long as we are alive, God will be working on us. She had been driving one day along a highway past a construction site, with miles of detours, cautionary signs, machinery and equipment. She finally came to the last sign which read: "End of construction. Thank you for your patience." This struck a chord within her. And so it's these very same words that you'll now find on her gravestone. We are all still works in progress. So do not let your sin or your failures define you. You are a precious, dearly loved child of the living God, who is even now being hand moulded by the ultimate master craftsman.

> *"...He who began a good work in you will carry it on to completion until the day of Christ Jesus."*
>
> Philippians 1:6

---

6. Mark 10:27

## *Remember where you've come from.*

As much as we shouldn't let sin define us, neither is it quite right to throw away all memory of it. I was helped in this by reading about an old preacher from England called Charles Simeon. He once wrote to a friend:

> *"With this sweet hope of ultimate acceptance with God, I have always enjoyed much cheerfulness before men; but I have at the same time laboured incessantly to cultivate the deepest humiliation before God... There are but two objects that I have ever desired for these 40 years to behold; the one, is my own vileness; and the other is, the glory of God in the face of Christ Jesus: and I have always thought that they should be viewed together... By this I seek to be, not only humble and thankful, but humbled in thankfulness, before my God and saviour continually."*[7]

*Charles Simeon*

For Simeon, the point of remaining, even enhancing one's awareness of your own sin, was not to weigh yourself down in some kind of self-beating way but to increase one's gratefulness and joy in God, by more fully appreciating what He has done and saved you from. One time when Jesus was invited to eat with a Pharisee, a women came along (who it seems had probably been a prostitute, but this isn't quite explicitly stated) and started weeping over Jesus' feet as he reclined at a table. She then proceeded to wipe them

---

7. Memoirs of the life of Charles Simeon: With a selection from his writings and correspondence, William Carus, 1801, p518-520

clean using her hair, before anointing them with some ointment she'd brought along. The Pharisee was not impressed saying to himself *"If this man were a prophet, he would have known who and what sort of woman this is who is touching him, for she is a sinner."*[8] Jesus knowing the man's thoughts responded with a story. *"A certain moneylender had two debtors. One owed five hundred denarii, and the other fifty. When they could not pay, he cancelled the debt of both. Now which of them will love him more?" Simon answered, "The one, I suppose, for whom he cancelled the larger debt." And he said to him, "You have judged rightly." Then turning toward the woman he said to Simon, "Do you see this woman? I entered your house; you gave me no water for my feet, but she has wet my feet with her tears and wiped them with her hair. You gave me no kiss, but from the time I came in she has not ceased to kiss my feet. You did not anoint my head with oil, but she has anointed my feet with ointment. Therefore I tell you, her sins, which are many, are forgiven—for she loved much. But he who is forgiven little, loves little."*[9] What we need to take away from this story is not some strange sense of others being lucky, who's been forgiven more than we have, and therefore love more. Now, as was stereotypical, the Pharisee thought of himself as being ok, more than that, as being a righteous person not needing forgiveness, or if so, just a little. We mustn't repeat the mistake ourselves, and perhaps even be envious of others with more dramatic conversion

---

8. Luke 7:39
9. Luke 7:41-47

stories. What we need is simply a greater, more thorough and precise knowledge of our personal failings.

Consider Formula 1 racing. You might mistakenly think that in the designing of these ultrafast cars, that every gram they can reduce the weight by without compromising the power or strength of the car is taken away. But that's not the case. Certainly, that might be the starting point, but the overall weight of the car is just one factor. Having made it as light as possible, they'll often go back and add weight back into particular areas for one specific purpose – balance. There's no point having all that power if it can't be controlled properly, and having a well-balanced vehicle is part of making it as good as it can be. Similarly, with us and sin, we serve ourselves best, not by throwing overboard any thought or memory of past sin, but by moving it from being a burden weighing us down, to being ballast. This keeps us balanced and able to revel in the power now available to us through the Holy Spirit, without becoming big-headed. It helps to keep us both humble and joyful in God. Just in case I'm misunderstood here, let me stress that I'm talking about the memory of past sin, not current sins being battled with. That should absolutely be dealt with and thrown overboard, leaving only the humbling memory.

## *Remember to rest and strive*

Rest in who God is and who He has declared you to be. Never try to earn anything before God, especially don't try to earn your salvation. If you want to try a route where you earn your own way and pay your own debt of sin, you'll always come up badly and ridiculously short. So be at peace knowing that you no longer owe any debt of sin. But be active, as you bask in your equally unpayable debt of love! We owe God everything, and so the only proper response is surely being willing to lay down anything and everything for Him as He may ask of us. To strive forwards seeking to lay hold of that for which His love laid hold of us. No longer living as slaves of sin, but instead slaves of righteousness,[10] with but one Lord – Jesus Christ, Son of God.

Walking with God, getting to know Him, and becoming the God-centred person He wants to transform you into, is not just one more job to add to the list, it is the reason you're alive. It's worth straining and striving for as we rest in Him. And so with this in mind, this is how I'd like to grow old – letting all else fall away, till all that remains is a man full of Godly faith, hope and love. Bringing glory to His name, belonging and identity to my soul, and gladly overflowing to bless others.

---

10. Rom 6:17-18

*"With this in mind, we constantly pray for you, that our God may make you worthy of his calling, and that by his power he may bring to fruition your every desire for goodness and your every deed prompted by faith. We pray this so that the name of our Lord Jesus may be glorified in you, and you in him, according to the grace of our God and the Lord Jesus Christ."*

2 Thess 1:11-12 NIV

~ 8 ~

# Daydreaming With God

> "...no eye has seen, nor ear heard, nor the heart of man imagined, what God has prepared for those who love him"
>
> *1 Cor 2:9*

Let me leave you with an extra thought that has long intrigued me. We're told that faith, hope and love will all still be significant and of value in the life to come. Now love's continuing role is immediately easy to see and understand, but what about faith and hope? Do we really still need faith (being certain of what we don't see) when we'll be able to see God face to face? Do we still need hope (the expectation of future good) when we've actually arrived at our ultimate and awesome future promised to us? What's the significance of these still being an important part of us? I can only speculate of course, but here's what I think may be the implication – activity. It's easy to think of the next life as one big and eternal retirement home. Certainly, that's what has come across to me at times when I've heard it spoken about? And of course, there are all those pictures out there of people floating around on clouds, maybe playing an instrument. Indeed, that's another possibility sometimes inferred – that eternity will be one long worship session. And while it's true that our future life will indeed be full of praising God, it's worth remembering that Paul, speaking to the church in Rome, spoke of our spiritual act of worship being in the way that we live and use our bodies (a living sacrifice).[1] How we praise God then will be no doubt even richer and more varied than the ways we worship Him now.

If I'm honest, none of these previous things mentioned has filled me with much eagerness or anticipation for our future life with God. Any singular thing done forever without end, however good it may be, ultimately fills me with weariness, if not dread. Admittedly this is probably not a great reaction inside of me, but it is the honest one. However, thinking about faith and hope continuing on through all time, starts to awaken my soul. That surely indicates, activity, discovery and growth? No longer with any fear or strife in the background, battling against evil in any form, but rather an enduring life of discovering God, and His creativeness. Of exploring new things, and learning. Of stepping out into the new with absolute faith, without even the slightest hint of fear in the background. Of a life where there is always the excitement of anticipation with something to look forward to, as well as fully appreciating what you already have and experience. A life where we will never exhaust the wonder, playfulness and imagination of our God.

We simply cannot imagine what God has in store for us. But that doesn't mean we shouldn't try. It just means whatever we can come up with in our puny minds will be utterly exceeded by the reality. So I invite you to do some 'daydreaming' with God. Ponder it, ask Him about it. Search the scriptures for what it does say about it (for some details are given). Then sit back and let your excitement grow for our future life with God, endeavouring to live now in the light of then.

---

1. Rom 12:1

www.ingramcontent.com/pod-product-compliance
Lightning Source LLC
Chambersburg PA
CBHW071631080526
44588CB00010B/1359